True State Trooper Stories

True State Trooper Stories

SGT. CHARLES A BLACK

Copyright © 2016 Sgt. Charles A Black
All rights reserved.

ISBN: 1535026626
ISBN 13: 9781535026628

5-28-1965   6-30-2000

    In 35 years I have seen a lot of changes from the name of the organization to the primary function.

    From hearses to ambulances to rescue units with EMT's. From paper list of stolen cars to computers. From no recorders to body cameras. From fist fights to gun fights.

    But human nature and the effects of drugs and alcohol remain the same.

Dedication

*This book is dedicated to my wife and children
who put up with my rotating shifts, missed
holidays and unpredictable hours.
You will never know how much I appreciate
your understanding and patience.
And to the fine troopers with whom
I was proud to serve. You always had my back.*

Contents

The Icy Hill ·1
Be Careful What You Wish For · · · · · · · · · · · · · ·3
In the cornfield ·4
Federal Agent Afraid of Speed · · · · · · · · · · · · · ·6
The Toughest Man I Ever Fought · · · · · · · · · · · ·8
"I Will Kill Myself and the Baby" · · · · · · · · · · · 11
Bob's Chair · 19
Ice Cream Cone Lost · 22
No need to Lecture · 24
Protest at the Capitol · 26
The Hole in the Floor· 28
The Finger · 31
Radar Stories · 33
You Can't Hurt Him · 35
You Move It · 37
You Never Know · 40
Where is the airplane? · · · · · · · · · · · · · · · · · · · 41
You Are a Nazi · 42
The Shovel · 44
The Night Before Christmas · · · · · · · · · · · · · · 45

Does Size Matter?······················47
Cut or Run?··························49
Car-Jacker on Foot·····················51
Not Your Typical Airline················56
How Dumb Can They Get?················58
How Did They Do That?·················60
Honor Among Thieves?··················62
High Speed Pursuit····················64
Hell Hath No Furry····················65
The Entertainer's Crew and the Carnies········67
Rocky Marciano (World Champ Boxer)·······70
The Great Flood of 1993················73
The Leg·····························77
The Law of Salvage····················80
Turkeys on the Road···················81
Three at a Time······················82
A Car Load·························86
Aliens Have Put a Radio in my Head········88
Ambulance/Hearse····················90
A Good Way to Start the Day?···········92
Backseat Fatality·····················97
Best Comebacks·····················99
The Boy Scout and the Drunk Driver······100
Death Notifications··················101
Grill Donor Program·················103
Iowa Jam·························104
Jeep Help?························106

Pilot Stories	107
Legal Intervention	109
I Told Him Not to Ask	113
The Iowa State Fair	116
My Most Unusual Thank You Letter	119
Animal Heads	121
Black Is Back	123
No I Will Walk Him Back	125
Is He Dead?	127
Over the Sidewalk and Through the Hedge	130
Thank You for the Ticket	131
The First Police Dog Leaves His Mark	132
Eye Tests	134
It Does Not Effect Anyone Else	137
Nighttime Illuminating Flare	139
It Takes a Licking	141
Prison Riot	142
I Just Called His Bluff	149
The Phone Call	151
The Blessed Virgin	153
Bozo the Clown	155
Fickle Fate	158
Secret Service Protection	159
The Motorcycle Toss	161
Darrell and the Pig	163
Push Bumpers	165

The Icy Hill

It was the winter 68-69 when we had had a lot of ice and it had stayed and built up. I was working the night shift and about 10 PM I got a call of a car in the ditch on a gravel road west of Ankeny. I was not familiar with the road but found it and started down it. The road was covered with about 1 inch of ice.

All of a sudden the road dropped down very steeply. At the bottom of the hill I could see a one-lane bridge. I could picture my car going across the bridge sideways and knew it would not fit. Grabbing the steering wheel I pushed the gearshift into neutral (in that car the engine idled fast enough to keep the back tires turning if you braked gently on ice) praying I could keep the car going straight.

Going down the hill braking gently. I had a death grip on the steering wheel, I passed the people standing on shoulder by the car in the ditch.

They watched me go by.

I kept the car straight and got across the bridge breathing again as I started up the other side I was pushing the gas pedal very softly repeating "come on, you can do it". Half way up I realized I had not put it back in gear.

I came to a stop short of the top of the hill thinking I might as well call a tow truck when I noticed the car start to slide down the hill backwards. *&$@! I knew I could not make it across the bridge that way and decided to just back it into the shallow ditch and get towed out. Embarrassing but not fatal.

I turned the wheel and dropped the backend into the ditch. To my surprise the front end swung around, the backend came out of the ditch and I was headed for the bridge again. This time I did not break but gave it some gas. Again repeating, "come on you can do it, you can do it".

Down the hill and some how across the bridge, past the people standing by their car and up the hill just making it.

After starting to breath again and prying my hands off the wheel I **Walked** back down to the people and told them I would call a tow truck for them. I wonder what they thought watching a patrol car go past them, up the other side, make a bootleg turn and go past them again.

I laugh at it now but I still wonder how I made it across that narrow bridge on a sheet of ice, **TWICE**.

Be Careful What You Wish For

I had stopped a young man for speeding on Highway 169 north of Adel one hot July day. As I was inspecting his license and other papers he said, "I wish I could ride around in a nice air-conditioned car."

While writing out the ticket in my patrol car, I ran a wanted and license check on him. I went back up to his car and told him, "I have good news and bad news. The good news is you're going to get a ride in a nice air-conditioned car. The bad news is you'll be wearing handcuffs and going to jail on an arrest warrant."

In the Cornfield

A hot summer night in August, I hear one of the troopers calls he is in pursuit of a stolen car. I start toward him. A minute later he call the driver lost control on a curve went into the ditch and the 2 subjects ran on foot into a cornfield. Myself and other help arrives and we surround the cornfield, No one wants to go walking through the cornfield in the heat the leaves on the corn scratching you arms and hitting you in the face.

Then the chief of police from a nearby small town where the car was stolen arrives. He has his dog

Rock with him. Now this is a time before we had trained police dogs Rock is just a big very friendly

German police dog that the chief has for company.

I have an Idea. We get Rock out of the car and get him to start barking, like his size he has a big loud bark.

I then get on the loud speaker and tell them come out or we will send the dogs in to get you.

In a few seconds I hear "don't send the dog we are coming out, just don't send the dogs". The two come out with their hands in the air and are arrested.

The chief stands there holding Rocks leash not to keep Rock from attacking but to keep him from licking them. We put one of the subjects in a patrol car and the chief offers to haul the second one.

I put him in front the chief's car and the chief puts Rock in the backseat.

We stand and talk for a minute and then they start for jail and I go back on patrol.

About 20 minutes later I get a message to call the jail for the chief. When I do he tells me the guy I put in his car was afraid of dogs. I could just picture friendly old Rock smelling and licking him while he quakes in terror. Then he tells "This guy wet my seat".

Sometimes you just got to say it I said "I guess he wasn't house broken".

Federal Agent Afraid of Speed

We were working a drug interdiction project on the interstate highway south of Des Moines on a warm summer day. It was a simple project. We had put up signs advising "**Police drug check point ahead be prepared to stop**".

Our aircraft was over the area and he would call us whenever a car or truck stopped or made a U-turn.

Both stopping and U-turns are illegal. We would then stop that car. The idea was to let the criminals sort themselves out for us. Four of us in marked cars that did the chasing down and stopping of the violators.

We each had a Drug Enforcement Agent with us and another unmarked car with two more drug agents in it behind us. It was working very well. In addition to drugs we were getting wanted people and suspended drivers.

The patrol car I was driving was capable of doing 140 MPH and had a digital read out speedometer. By pushing a button it would change from MPH to KPH. So 120 MPH would be over 200 KPH.

One of the Federal Drug Agents out of the Omaha office was riding with me. He reached down and pulled his seat belt tighter and put his hands on the dash and armrest to brace himself.

This was too good a chance to pass up. When we had finished a traffic stop, which had turned out to be a driver with a revoked license. When we got back to the starting point I reached over to adjust the radio and pushed the button to change from miles per hour to kilometers per hour on the speedometer.

When it was our turn to chase the next car down I ran the car up over 120 MPH and waited. I could see him pulling on the seat belt and bracing himself again. Finally he glanced over and looked at the speedometer. I could hear him suck in air and see his face lose its color. I did not say a word but went about making the traffic stop.

The backup car of drug agents pulled up and I went about the business of issuing a citation and getting consent to search the car.

Some drugs were found and I turned the suspect over to the agents.

As I prepared to leave I looked for my rider. He was seated in the back seat of the agent's car and informed me that he planned to stay there. I was to find another backup and he was not going to ride with me again. I can see him back in Omaha trying to convince the other agents "that crazy Trooper was going 200 MPH."

The Toughest Man I Ever Fought

George was a drinker and a fighter. Sober, he was a nice guy, but drunk he was an animal. When the call came in that George was in a bar drunk and fighting, or getting ready to fight, we all went. With George it made no difference how badly he was hurt; if he could get up, he kept coming. He was the only man I know of who was charged with Mayhem twice. He once bit a guy's ear off and another man's nose off. He would fight one person or groups, and he almost always started the fight. We would fight him all the way from the bar to the jail cell. In the morning, he would go to court, pay the fine, and go to work.

One night George walked over to a group of four motorcycle gang members in a bar and kept insulting them until they took him on. They gave him a pretty good beating. Two weeks later he was back in a fight again. This went on for the five years I was there.

Then, one Saturday night a call came in that George was in a fight in one of the local bars. Four of us responded with a Deputy entering the bar first with me right behind him, followed by two other officers. George was standing at the back of the bar behind a pool table. He made a serious mistake – he was holding a pool cue like a baseball bat. Now he was armed with a deadly weapon. The deputy stopped and pulled out his service revolver, a Colt Python .357 Magnum with a six-inch barrel – a very impressive weapon.

The place got real quiet as O'Riley leveled his weapon at George across the pool table and said, "George, drop it or I will drop you." Just to add emphasis, he cocked the Python's hammer. You could have heard a pin drop.

George looked down the barrel of that gun, hesitated, then dropped the pool cue, turned and put his hands against the wall. We cuffed him and took him to jail without any problems. I decided right then that I would never fight George again. I might shoot him, but I wouldn't fight him again.

Two weeks later George got into a fight at a strip club where the bouncers used clubs and saps. They hospitalized him for six weeks and I believe caused some brain damage (or maybe fixed some). After that, George's fighting days were over. I would see him around once in a while, but no more fight calls.

A couple of years later I was talking to one of the deputies who told me he ran across George and they had a conversation. George had told him, "I know some of you guys would have shot me, but that Deputy, he *really* wanted to shoot me."

Actually George was wrong. *Many* police officers and civilians he had beaten up also wanted to shoot him and I was always surprised someone had not shot him.

A few months after George's beating at the strip club, the bar was closed due to numerous law suits filed because of the bouncers.

"I Will Kill Myself and the Baby"

The patrol car radio tone goes off to get everyone's attention and the dispatcher starts: *"Wanted for murder in Illinois. "John Wayne Govia". Driving a 1985 blue Thunderbird, Illinois license 123AXJ. He will be accompanied by his one-year-old son. Govia has threatened to kill his son and himself if stopped by the police. He left Chicago approximately three hours ago, possibly en root westbound on I-80."*

I figure if he keeps coming west, he should be here in about three hours. However, criminals seldom do what I plan for them to do. We continue patrol, working on the drinking driver project. But in the back of my mind is the question: If we do find him, how do we handle it? If I do try to stop him, will he kill the child? I know I can't let a man wanted for murder get away. And I know that decision, if it comes, will be mine.

About three hours later, one of the troopers about 15 miles west calls in and runs a registration check on an Iowa license plate. The plate is registered to a white Toyota, but the trooper tells the dispatcher that the plate is on a 1985 blue Thunderbird and to check with the Illinois State Police to see if they have any additional information on the car wanted in the murder in Illinois. The trooper was stopped in an I-80 rest area using the pay phone when the Thunderbird pulled in, spotted him, then pulled out without stopping.

I am riding with one of my troopers and we start west in pursuit at over 100 miles per hour. I am sure this is the car we are looking for. In a few minutes the dispatcher calls us and tells us the car has a Chicago Cubs bumper sticker and a radio station bumper sticker, which matches the car we are pursuing.

As my adrenaline level goes up, so does our speed. I call the trooper behind the car and request his status. He says they are going west doing 55 miles per hour. My stomach starts to knot up. I have the dispatcher call the troopers west of the suspect's location in the next post and get them started our way. I contact local sheriff and police departments ahead of us and have them go to I-80.

Now I know I will have to make the decision of what to do and if I choose wrong, someone may die, but I have to do something. The decisions I have to make in a split-second will be judged by others in leisure if it turns out badly. Part of me wishes I did not have to make the decisions and part of me says this is what I am paid to do. You make the decisions and you take the heat or the glory.

After what seems like a lifetime, we catch up to the T-bird and one of my troopers and two of the local police are on the highway ahead of us. I tell them to pull out and stay ahead of us. If "Govia" decides to try to outrun us when we attempt to stop him, they can block the road for us. Two other troopers catch up to us.

What do I do now? I have enough help, so it is up to me now to make the call. My heart is hammering, my stomach is tight, and the adrenaline is running full bore. I have to sound calm on the radio; if I don't, the troopers will catch my panic. I take a deep breath and call it: "We will try to stop him."

We pull up behind him and turn on the red lights on the patrol car. What will happen now? Probably the thing I least expected. "Govia" pulls onto the shoulder and stops the T-bird. Then I can see he is sitting in the car holding a pistol to his right temple and he has the baby on his lap. He just sits there with the gun to his head. I have him stopped and now I have two objectives: save the baby and, if I can, save him as well.

I approach the rear of the car, my gun drawn and pointed at him using his car for cover. I start yelling at him to "talk to me." It works. He starts talking to me, but I have trouble hearing him. I tell him, "Open the passenger door. I will be able to hear you and we can talk without shouting." He does it!

Now I have a better chance of grabbing the baby if I get a chance. He is telling me: "It wasn't my fault – "Pedro" made me shoot him. It was self-defense. I will not go to jail!" I keep him talking to me saying that I understand and that I have talked to the police in Illinois and they just want to talk to him about the self-defense. This goes on for what seems like hours.

Then he says, "I can't go to jail," and lowers the pistol from his head to his lap where the baby is. I can't see it or what he's doing with it. I make an instant decision that I cannot take a chance he will kill the baby. I will have to shoot him and it will have to be head shot to kill him instantly.

I rest my gun on the car and cock the hammer. Suddenly everything slows down like it is in slow motion. My senses become so acute I can feel the trigger as it slides along the slide plates. I can see his head in my sights. Everyone around me is moving in slow motion. The trigger passes the slack point and now it only takes four to six pounds of pressure to drop the hammer and he dies. I can hear the blood hammering in my ears.

Then his left hand comes up with the gun in it and he puts it to the other side of his head. I release the pressure on the trigger. I cannot believe it did not go off.

We start talking again and he tells me that he wants to believe me, but he can't. I realize he really does want to believe me and maybe I can use that. I start a new tact with him. "John", if we could talk face-to-face you could see that I'm very serious. But I can't come up to the car door while you still are holding the gun in your hand. If you will lay the gun down on the seat, then I can come up and talk to you face-to-face and you can see I am serious." I repeat this a few more times and he finally says "okay" and puts the gun down in the passenger seat.

"Okay, John, that's great," I say. "Now if you will put your hands on the steering wheel so I can see you don't have the gun I will come up and we can talk face-to-face." He puts his hands on the steering wheel.

"Okay, John, now I am coming up to the door. Just relax and we will talk now, okay?"

When I get to the door I see his hands on the steering wheel and the gun in the passenger seat. I say to him, "John, do you see those guys across the road there?" As he turns to look, I grab the gun and get out of the door, moving to the back of the car while shouting that I have the gun and for someone to get the baby. Someone grabs the baby and two troopers grab John and handcuff him.

I am at the back of the car and my legs are shaking so badly I have to lean against the car. My heart is pounding and I am breathing like I have been running a race. But this passes quickly as I still have a lot of work to do. Someone has called the dispatcher to report "one in custody." Still leaning against the back of the car I tell Trooper Stiles to take John back to his car and read him his Miranda rights and tape record it all.

My mouth feels like it is full of cotton, my heart is still hammering, but it is slowing down. I go back to the car and John has just finished telling how and why he shot him five times. Now, as I have just gotten into the car, I ask him to repeat his story, still on tape. I have the T-bird towed to the evidence lot and tagged while I retain custody of the gun.

We start for the jail and I tell the driver to stop at the gas station at the interchange and I will buy us all some pop. I go in and get three cans of Pepsi and as I return to the car, one of the cans ruptures spraying pop all over. I wonder if I still have that much tension in me since that is the only time it has ever happened to me.

John is booked and the baby is turned over to Child Protective Services.

Post Script:
When I talk to Illinois detectives, they tell me that John shot Pedro five times in the back while Pedro was running away. I go to Illinois for the start of the pre-trial and identify the gun I took from John. His taped confession is challenged. In Illinois you must tell a suspect he is being tape recorded – in Iowa you do not. However, the judge rules that the confession is admissible. Before the trial begins John hangs himself in the jail.

Post Post Script:
When we check the radio logs, we find that the whole incident took nine minutes.

I received the Departments Award for Bravery and took part in a reenactment of the incident on "Real Stories of the Highway Patrol"

Receiving the Department Award for Bravery

Sgt. Charles A Black

Black re-enacts incident on cable TV's 'True Stories'

Patrolman negotiates for the life of child, honored for bravery

By PHIP ROSS
Staff Writer

DES MOINES -- Former Shenandoah resident Charles Black, a sergeant with the Iowa State Patrol in Des Moines, was featured Monday night in a segment of the cable program "True Stories of the Highway Patrol."

Black, who graduated from Shenandoah High School in 1959, re-enacted an April 14, 1987, incident involving a fleeing murderer from Illinois who had kidnapped a 2-year-old and threatened to kill himself and the child.

Black, who spoke by phone from the patrol's District I office in West Des Moines, received the department's Award for Bravery after the incident in 1987, and appeared Monday in the latter part of the program titled "Heroes of the Highway Patrol."

Black said the event does not stand out among his other experiences. He has two scrapbooks he has used to keep track of his many unusual or dangerous experiences.

"They look for interesting re-enactments, and I guess that was one," he said, adding that the program's representation was condensed, but "pretty good."

CHARLES BLACK

The incident began when the fugitive, John Patrick Govia, shot his stepson five times and kidnapped a 2-year-old boy. Before heading west on Interstate 80, Govia called a relative and said if the "police stopped him he'd kill himself and the youngster," said Black, a 29-year veteran of the patrol.

Despite the plates being changed on Govia's vehicle, patrol officers identified the car and were able to stop it about 25 miles west of Des Moines. "He puts the pistol up to his own head, saying, he'll kill himself, he'll kill himself," Black said. "I go up to the car and start talking to him ... I finally convince him to unlock the passenger side door."

As Black negotiated with the man, the 2-year-old was on his lap. At one point, the man lowered the gun from his head and Black's concern shifted to the child. But the man raised the gun to the other side of his head. "My primary concern was getting the kid out of there alive," he said.

When Black got the man to lay the gun down on the seat and put his hands on the steering wheel, he grabbed the gun while another patrolman removed the child. "We had to do what we had to do to get the baby out of the car ... to make sure he didn't carry through on his threat," Black said.

"It lasted about seven minutes, but I would've sworn it lasted for 15 or 20," he added.

After the program aired, Black's mother Dorothy of Shenandoah said she knew it was her son. Comparing it to other segments of the show that are shot live, the re-enactments are much better quality, she said. "Boy, I could recognize him immediately," she said. "It was sure a good, clear colored picture."

Govig was extradited to Illinois and was convicted of murder. He hung himself in a county jail before sentencing.

Bob's Chair

If you don't believe that Methamphetamine ("Meth") can make you stupid, think about this: the ingredients are white gas, anhydrous ammonia (farm fertilizer), starting-ether, and lithium batteries – not the kind of stuff I want to put in my body. And if you don't cook it correctly, it will explode. The fumes are toxic in a closed room. What part of this sounds like a good idea? Here is an example of the debilitating effects of meth.

A man went into a Wal-Mart store and purchased everything they sell that can be used to cook meth, then paid for it with a personal check, supplying a driver's license as I.D. The store employees, trained to watch for situations like this, called us. We then used the information to obtain a search warrant for the residence – an old farmhouse the man was renting. We decided to wait until the next morning to serve the warrant, figuring all would be home and asleep.

When we raided the house, we found three women and six children, but not the two males we were looking for. I checked the outbuildings and found a sort of office in one of them. I also noticed a set of fresh car tracks in the morning dew that led around a fence and down the side of a corn field. I decided to get my patrol car and follow them.

I smelled ether, so I knew I was close when suddenly I came upon an open area at the end of a few corn rows. There were the men cooking a batch of meth. I was as surprised as they were. I saw two rifles on the ground by the men. Fortunately, while meth is supposed to speed you up, its continued use slows your mind down. By the time their brains had processed the information, I was out of my car with my gun drawn. I had them lay face-down on the ground and called on the radio, "I could use some help back here."

The response was, "Where are you?" I had not told anyone where I was going – not a good idea.

Help showed up and we arrested them. One of the suspects, named Bob, wanted to know how we knew about them. I told him we were tipped off by an "informant." I knew that would make him suspicious of his friends. I wasn't about to tell him that Wal-Mart had given us the lead. They were transported to the jail and booked.

I knew that in a few days they would be released on bond and I assumed that shortly thereafter they would be back cooking meth again. I returned to the barn office and over a nice office chair there was a sign that said "Bob's Chair: Sit in it and you die." There was also a Polaroid camera on the desk. I couldn't resist. I called one of the other troopers, sat in Bob's chair, put my feet up on Bob's desk, and had the trooper take my photo, which I left on Bob's desk.

I kept track of the house for a few weeks and on an early Sunday morning had one of our Patrol aircraft fly over the house at first light to see if I could catch them back out cooking more meth. Sure enough. I did, they did, and I arrested them again, though this time I took some backup with me.

Bob didn't mention the photo, but then he probably didn't remember me either. As I said, meth screws up your mind.

Ice Cream Cone Lost

I was on patrol a warm summer evening and I decided o get an ice cream cone. I had gone about 2 blocks hen I saw a car come up an incline on a side road and stop at the stop sign. The car then slowly rolled backward until one tire went off in the ditch. I turned my patrol car around and came up behind the car. I could see the driver sitting in the drivers seat.

I put my ice cream cone in the cup holder and walked up to he drivers side of the car. He was sitting behind the steering wheel continuing the movements of "driving". The car was stuck in the ditch yet he continued to "drive" like he still going down he road unaware that the car was not moving.

When I got closer I could smell the alcohol and knew what the problem was. I tapped him on the shoulder and asked "Are you having trouble?". He slowly turned, looked at me up and down for a short time then he said "no". He turned back to the steering, shifted into second gear and started "driving" again. I walked back to the patrol car, called for a tow truck to impound the car and tossed my new, now melted, ice cream cone into the ditch.

I walked back up to the car he was still "driving". I opened the drivers door.

The driver looked at me with a very confused look on his face turned back to his "driving" and turned on the windshield wipers. He looked at me again as if he was trying to figure out how I could be standing there while he was traveling down the road.

I took him by the arm and said "Time to go". He let me assist him out of the car and walk him back to he patrol car. All this time he kept turning his head and looking at me with that confused look.

I took him to the jail and he just sat in car looking straight ahead and then he would look at me, turn back and reach up like he was trying to figure out where the steering wheel went.

In the jail he just kept looking around trying figure out where he was and where his car went.

His Blood Alcohol level tested .340. Better than 4X the legal limit.

No wonder he was disoriented!

No need to Lecture

While patrolling on the interstate highways some times I liked to get in the slow lane and drive about 10 MPH under the speed limit.

This way I can check the cars that pass me and the ones that do not pass me. I have had people pass me not wearing their seat belt, with expired license plates and even speeding. In one case a man passed me not wearing his seat belt. I stopped him when I ran a check on him he had a warrant for his arrest and his driver's license was suspended.

I remember a car that came up behind and followed me for a few miles. I could see in my rear view mirror his wife talking to him. Then he passed me and I noticed he was not wearing a seat belt.

When I got to the car window and told him why I had stopped him his wife said: "I told you so". I told him back to the patrol car and wrote him a warning. I told him "My philosophy is a man will take a butt chewing if you don't cite him. If you cite him he gets no chewing out. Now with a warning you can chew him out a little".

"I am not going to say a word. I am sure your wife will take care of that for me". He said "Yes and when we go out with friends she will love telling this story".

Protest at the Capitol

During the era of the Viet Nam War protests, the Patrol was often assigned to protect citizens and property against rioting, such as at the University of Iowa in Iowa City. At the time I was assigned to Post #1 and after the first day of protest duty in Iowa City, we were told to return to Des Moines, so we thought our work was done. When we got back to Des Moines we learned there was going to be a protest at the Iowa State Capitol Building and we were assigned to protect it.

When we assembled at the Capitol, the large crowd of protesters was gathered on the west side of the building listening to speakers. Of course the news services were there in full force as well. Our group of twelve officers was assigned to the porch area just outside the west doors at the top of the steps overlooking the protesters. As we watched, one of the speakers urged the crowd to "go see the governor." (The governor was not there, but the speaker must not have known that.)

So the crowd started up the steps toward us. Twelve troopers looking into a crowd of over a thousand was not good odds. It seemed to us that the sensible course of action was to retreat into the building and lock the doors. But we were too late – the people inside the building had already locked the doors and were not about to open them for us.

Now what to do? What do you do when you can't retreat and you face overwhelming odds? You bluff.

Quickly we formed a line at the top of the stairs looking down at the approaching protesters. We stood in a straight parade rest formation blocking their way, each one of us trying to look confident that no protester would get by us.

The crowd stopped for a moment, but I was sure they would restart soon. Then one of the speakers came forward and talked the crowd into going back down. We stood there not moving (except for shaking knees) until they had returned to the bottom of the steps where they listened to more speeches. The crowd eventually broke up and left.

Then we turned back to the doors. (Those inside had a good reason not to unlock them now.) Finally, someone unlocked them and we all went inside and collapsed into chairs.

The moral is: Never turn your back on a building full of politicians.

The Hole in the Floor

I was sent to a report of a burglar alarm going off at a residence. It was during a snow storm so no backup was available. The front door was open but no one answered my knocks or yells. I could here a voice in the house but it was to weak to understand. I entered the home with my gun in my hand but pointed at the floor. As I was walking down the hall yelling police as I walked past the alarm box it went off with a loud siren. I jumped and as I did I jerked the trigger and the gun went off shooting a hole in the floor.

I knew I was going to get ribbed at the Christmas Party where I was the M.C. so I wrote this poem and read it at the start. That stopped it before itstarted.

While working on a snowy day

Came a call from a County, far way

A burglar alarm was ringing away

And they had no deputy to send, what can I say

They were all busy and respond they could not

They were at the jail guarding the coffee pot

So I answered the call, I looked quite dashing

The outside alarm light was flashing

A check showed, open was the front door
I knew it was up to me to do more

Stepping in the door and yelling ahead

I received no answer - the house was dead

Entering the house I again gave a call

Then, I heard a whispered voice down the hall

Now it was serious and no longer fun

Moving down the hall I drew my gun

Suddenly from nowhere a siren did start

Causing me to miss a few beats of my heart

Finger on the trigger and ready to score

With a quick jerk – I shot a hole in the floor

The voice was clear - he did not like it one bit

Now he is in therapy.

All he will say is "Oh shit".

> • State Patrol Sgt. Charles Black was checking out a burglary-alarm call at the Waukee home of Jean Ann Kelly when he accidentally fired his gun.
>
> "As he approached a bathroom doorway on his left, the siren alarm suddenly started to blast away, causing him to jump. He then squeezed the trigger of his handgun, discharging it into the floor," said a report describing the incident.
>
> The bullet caused $418 in damage to the

The Finger

It was near the end of a long shift on a hot summer day. I was a mile from home, looking forward to a cold glass of iced tea and getting rid of the vest and gun belt. As I turned a corner near home I happened to glance over at a car stopped at the stop sign. The driver was giving me the finger! Well, my plans for home would be delayed. I made a U-turn and dropped in behind him as he turned the corner. Lo and behold, he had expired California license plates on his car. I turned on the red lights and pulled him over.

I walked up to the car and asked the driver, "Were you trying to get my attention back there?"

"No," he replied.

"Well, you did," I said, "and I noticed your license plates are expired. License and registration please." He gave me a California driver's license and expired registration.

As I started to write the citation, I asked for his present address and he gave me a local one.

"How long have you lived there?" I asked.

"About four months," he answered.

"Well, you're past the deadline to have an Iowa driver's license," I informed him.

As I was writing the citations, I noted the name of the lien holder on the car was GMAC Finance. I wondered if the reason he was driving with expired plates was because he was not making his car payments and didn't want GMAC Finance to know where he was living. The next morning I called the local GMAC office and asked if they were looking for that car. In a few minutes I received a return call that they were, indeed, looking for that car.

"I'll tell you where the car is, but you have to do one thing for me," I told them. "Please tell the owner where you got the information." Maybe next time he waves at a police officer, I hope he's learned his lesson and waves with his whole hand.

Radar Stories

When I was starting out as a Highway Patrolman, the radar was a box mounted on a tripod that you set up alongside the road with a cable leading back to another box that contained the readout in miles per hour. We set it up in such a way that each patrol car could pull up to the box and watch the readout of the speed of the cars going by. When a speeding car drove by, you chased it down. Then the next patrol car pulled up to the box and did he same. I saw this happen one evening: One of the troopers pulled up to the box and a car went by traveling at 100 mph. The trooper took off so fast after the violator that his spinning wheels on the gravel shoulder moving the back end of the patrol car sideways and the back bumper hooked the radar cable, jerking the box off the jack-stand and dragging it down the road. When he turned onto the pavement of the highway, the control and radar boxes bounced and sparked along the pavement following the patrol car. We called on the radio to get him stopped, but by then the damage had been done. That was the end of running radar at night.

Then we got the first portable radar units that mounted on the outside of the window of the patrol car behind the driver, pointed toward oncoming traffic.

As you drove down the highway, the unit clocked and recorded the speed of oncoming cars. On one occasion, a trooper had clocked a speeder and written him a citation. The trooper returned to his patrol car, followed shortly by the driver who wanted to argue. The driver stood talking to the trooper while standing in front of the radar unit.

After giving the man the chance to voice his concern, the trooper finally grew tired of the argument which was going nowhere and told the man, "If you stand in front of that radar much longer, it may sterilize you." The man turned around, ran to his car, and left. End of discussion.

You Can't Hurt Him

There were three of us in the office doing reports when the call came in there was a robbery in progress at the gas station right across the street. The suspect, wearing a yellow shirt and blue jeans, had *r*eportedly left on foot northbound on a side street, so we all took off in pursuit. I spotted him about three blocks away just walking down the street. We surrounded him with guns drawn, ordering him to get on the ground. One look at him and I could tell he was drugged up. After repeated orders to get on the ground, he finally got down on his hands and knees, but no further.

We decided we would have to approach him to put him the rest of the way down to restrain him.

The first thing I did was check his belt and, sure enough, there was a gun stuck in it. I removed the weapon and handed it back to a deputy to hold. Then two of us each grabbed an arm and put him into an arm bar compliance restraint. His front end went down, but not his knees. I put more pressure on his arm, which is painful. But instead of going down, he started struggling.

Anyone can get out of a pain compliance hold if he is willing to pay the price or is under the influence of drugs or alcohol and can't feel it. (Later, we learned that he had just shot up with heroin and was one week out of prison where he'd spent his time lifting weights.) So he was willing to pay the price and broke our hold. Now there were three or four of us trying to cuff him and the fight was really on with everyone twisting arms and legs struggling to get him cuffed. Finally, after an exhausting struggle and a lot of help, we got his hands cuffed and legs shackled.

At this point I noticed a lot of blood on the suspect's shirt, thinking it was his. Then I realized that the blood was *mine*. I had a cut over my eye that would require eight stitches to close.

The next day when the jailer brought the suspect down to court, the drugs had worn off and the guy could hardly walk he was so sore.

So was I.

You Move It

On a bright and clear sunny summer day I was called to the scene of a motorcycle accident. The motorcycle carrying two people had run off the roadway into a six-foot ditch. The young man who was driving had minor injuries and was walking, but his female passenger said she could not feel her arms or legs. The county ambulance was on its way, but I felt that we needed the Life Flight helicopter air ambulance and requested our dispatch to call them.

The First Responders arrived, followed by the county ambulance and crew. I told the EMT that Life Flight had been called and he said, "We will see about that," and walked off. He was obviously mad that we had called the helicopter. They had parked the ambulance on the road near the scene and were working in the ditch. When the helicopter arrived, I asked the EMT to please move the ambulance so the helicopter could land as it was the only good landing spot within a half-mile.

He gave me a dirty look and said, "I'm busy. If you want it moved, you move it."

It was a "count to ten" moment. I really wanted to tell him what a jerk he was being.

I walked back up to the road, called another nearby trooper, and told him to get his car and come pick me up.

I drove the ambulance about a half-mile down the road and parked it off the road in a farm drive, then rode back to the accident scene.

After the girl was loaded in the helicopter and it took off, I could see the EMT looking for the ambulance. When he spotted it down the road, he looked at me. I was taking measurements with the other trooper. He walked up to the other trooper and asked for a ride to the ambulance. The trooper, who had seen what had happened, told him, "Check with the Sargent to see if it's okay."

The EMT finally did approach me and asked for a ride. My response was, "We're busy right now, but if you wait I should be done in twenty minutes or so and can do it then."

As I expected, the next day he had his boss call our office to complain. I suggested to my Lieutenant that he and I go and meet with the EMT and his boss at the ambulance barn. (I didn't want the EMT claiming he could not leave the ambulance in case of a call.)

When we got there he was nervous. We all sat down and I explained what had happened. Very simply I had asked him to move the ambulance so we could land the helicopter and he told me that if I wanted it moved, then I should move it, which I did. I wanted to be sure I parked it in a safe place, far enough away that the wind from the helicopter didn't throw rocks and debris and break a window. I also wanted to be sure the ambulance was safely off the roadway.

The head of the ambulance service apologized for bothering us and thanked me for looking out for his equipment. When we were leaving, the EMT tried to follow us out, but his boss called him back and told him, "Close the door."

You Never Know

When I was working as a Trooper, I saw this work in an interesting way. I had been called to a domestic situation. I arrived at the same time as a deputy sheriff and we could hear the sound of a fight with a woman calling for help.

When we entered the home, we found a man holding a woman on the floor and hitting her. We pulled him off and as we were struggling to get him handcuffed I could hear the woman behind me swearing. I could also feel her hitting my back. Help arrived and the situation was put under control.

Someone asked me how badly I was hurt. It turned out that the woman had not been hitting me, but actually had a small kitchen knife and was stabbing me in the back. I was saved by my bulletproof vest.

The last thing I expected when I left for work that day was that someone I had just saved from a beating would attack me with a knife. What saved me was the habit I had of putting on that vest every day.

Where is the airplane?

A trooper I worked with tells this story about working speed enforcement with the patrol aircraft in western Iowa.

He had stopped a car for speeding and the driver protested. He told the Trooper I do not believe there is an aircraft up there".

This was during the cold war and the Offutt Air Force Base with the B-52 Intercontinental Bombers was just across the river. They practiced low level flying in the area.

The trooper called the pilot to come lower and show the driver he was there.

The Pilot responded that he had just been instructed to by air traffic control to leave the area as a B-52 was coming by.

The trooper went back and told the driver the plane would make a low pass in a minute.

Right on time here comes the B-52 about 100 feet above the ground and close to them the roar is deafening as it passes over.

The driver said "OK." stopped protesting and signed the citation.

You Are a Nazi

I had stopped a subject driving 80 mph in a 60 mph zone and weaving in his lane. As I was putting him through the sobriety test, and he was failing, he decided that I was a Nazi and this was like the concentration camps. He started calling me "The Feuhrer." He told me he had a bug on his person and that his family was recording everything and tracking him. (If I had a relative like him, I would want to know where he was so I could be someplace else.) I didn't tell him that I was also recording everything on the patrol car camera. I told him he was under arrest for speeding and drunk driving. Then he decided I was a Communist and that this was just like Russia. When I cuffed him and put him in the car, he started again about how I was both a Communist and a Nazi.

It was obvious he was not the sharpest knife in the drawer. I decided to have a little fun and give him a history lesson at the same time. I said, "You're going to have to decide, am I a Nazi or a Communist? I can't be both because the Nazis fought the Communists until the Communists from Russia and the Allied Forces destroyed the Nazis. Now which is it, Communist or Nazi?"

This stopped him cold for a minute. Then he said, "Nazi."

I continued, "I can't be a Nazi. They were all killed in World War Two."

Then he decided I was a Communist.

"I can't be a Communist. I am a Methodist." He thought about this and was quiet the rest of the trip.

The Shovel

I was helping with the investigation of a truck accident in which two people were killed.

A straight truck had run off the road, hit a bridge support, and came to rest on a guard rail. Then the truck caught fire. The passenger was thrown out, but the driver was killed on impact. His body was pinned in the truck's burning cab.

After the fire was put out, the tow trucks tried to lift the wreckage off the guard rail in order to remove the driver's body. The cab split open and the body fell out. Someone got a body bag and I went to get a shovel.

As I returned with the shovel, one of the other troopers asked me, "What are you going to do with that shovel after you've used it for this?"

I answered, "Put it back in the trunk of your car. That's where I got it."

When the job was completed, I walked back toward the parked cars. The other trooper followed right behind me saying, "Do not put that in my trunk.

I finally had to tell him it was not his shovel.

The Night Before Christmas

(This poem is biased on my experiences one Christmas Eve)

It was the night before Christmas and all over the state.
The Troopers all over were out working late.

The carolers sang "peace on earth good will to men".
And the Troopers waited for their shift to end.

When what to their wondering eyes should appear.
But a car load of drunks singing and drinking beer.

Oh, well they said this is just fine
I didn't expect to get home on time.

The drunks were all booked safe in the jail.
They were soon on the phone trying to make bail.

Then the call came a bad accident had occurred
How they hate to get that word.

Sgt. Charles A Black

Away to the scene they flew like a flash
The caller was right it was a bad crash.

The Trooper picked up a small child and looked to the sky.
And in a whispered prayer he said
"please don't let him die".

At the hospital he was told the child would be all right.
And walked out knowing it has been a great night.

And I heard him exclaim as he drove out of sight.
"Merry Christmas to all and to all a good night".

Does Size Matter?

It was four o'clock in the morning. I was working the 10 pm. to 7 am. shift and had just stopped into the office with two other troopers. As we were talking I looked out the window at the Interstate highway and observed a truck and a motorcycle come down the off-ramp and stop on the shoulder. The truck driver walked back and began talking to the motorcyclist, who was a big man about six-feet, four-inches tall, weighing 250 pounds, and very angry. The truck driver, about five-feet, ten-inches tall and about 180 pounds, was trying to calm him down without much success.

I said, "I think we need to get out there," just as the big guy drew back to hit the smaller man.

Before he could complete the punch, the smaller truck driver hit him twice and down he went.

By the time we got there, the big guy was starting to come around. I recognized him as someone I had encountered two weeks before when he and two of his buddies had assaulted a young man at Clear Water Beach, but the young man had been too scared to file charges. It turned out that the motorcycle rider thought the truck had cut him off up on the Interstate.

The truck driver said, "I tried to explain to him that I didn't see him and tried to apologize. But then he tried to hit me, so I defended myself."

The motorcycle rider wanted to file charges. I told him, "That's not going to happen, but if you want, you can go to the County Attorney on Monday. But this out-of-state driver will be long gone by then."

I could see the motorcycle rider starting to think, "Well, the cops are here, so I can sneak a punch and they will keep him from hitting back." I could also see that the truck driver was preparing for just that scenario. The motorcyclist drew his fist back, but before he got any further, the truck driver hit him twice and down the big man went, blood gushing from his nose and mouth.

Again, he wanted to file assault charges. I explained there were three witnesses that saw him attempt to throw the first punch, so that he would be booked after we took him to the hospital.

In talking to the truck driver I learned that he had been a sparring partner for Sonny Liston, former world heavy weight boxing champion. Speed and knowing how to punch, not size, won this one

Cut or Run?

This incident occurred while I was working the State Fair. One evening as another trooper and I were entering the midway (carnival) area, we saw a young man running toward us being chased by two other men, who were yelling at him to stop. Looking at the young man more closely, I saw he was carrying a knife. As he ran by us, I tripped him, we pinned him to the ground, and I took the knife away from him. The two men who were chasing him explained what had happened.

They were walking through the midway with their wives (one of whom was very pregnant) and passed the young man with the knife who was with three of his friends. One of these friends bumped into the pregnant lady. The lady's husband said, "Hey, watch it."

The man's response was, "Keep the bitch out of my way," and he waited for the husband to answer. The husband didn't say a word – he just punched the man and laid him out cold.

At this point, the young man we had stopped pulled the knife and said, "I'll cut you," while displaying the knife, no doubt expecting the lady's husband to back off. Big mistake.

The husband moved toward him. The knife holder had to decide to either cut or run and he chose to run, which is where we came in.

As we were getting this story, the other three young "toughs" walked up, two of them helping the one who had been punched and who was still unsteady. The husband who had punched him, it turned out, was a roofer, so he was in very good shape, along with the fact that he had boxed in Golden Gloves competition, so he knew how to punch. The young man with the knife was booked for carrying a dangerous weapon with intent to cause injury (since he had threatened the husband, telling him that he would cut him and pulled the knife – just before he ran). That is why I still have the knife.

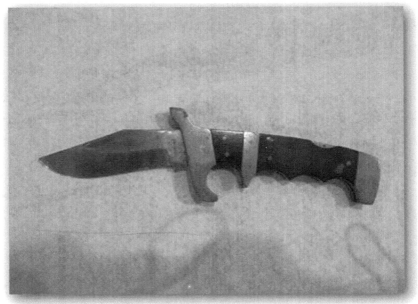

The knife he used in this story

Car-Jacker on Foot

It's a hot summer day in Iowa and I'm patrolling Interstate 80. Up ahead I spot a car on the shoulder with two men changing the flat front tire. So, I pull in behind them to see if they need any help. But I'm careless – I do not call in my location or the car's license plate number. After all, it's just a stalled car, right? Well, I'm about to find out just how wrong that assumption is.

As I get out and walk toward the car, I observe the trunk lock as been punched out. This is not a good sign. Continuing on, I look into the car and observe that the steering wheel lock has been broken. There is the barrel of a pistol sticking out from under the driver's seat and a long gun wrapped in a blanket in the back seat. (I think, "Way to go – now how do you plan to handle this one?")

I decide to bluff my way through it. I can see they are wearing T-shirts and shorts, so no place to hide a gun on them. One of them walks back to meet me and I ask if they are having trouble. "Yes," he says. They have a flat and no spare tire. I tell them to just take the flat off and I'll take them to a station to get it fixed. (Oh, yeah, I'll get his flat fixed. You go ahead and take it off while I have my dispatcher call the station to be ready.)

The talker returns to the flat tire and I carefully back up to my patrol car, get in, pick up the microphone and give my location and the car's license number (which I should have done in the first place) and request backup. The talker starts walking back toward me. I get out to meet him and he says he has the title to the car and will get it if I want to see it. He starts to open the car door. I know there are guns in the car and I know that the game is over.

I draw my service revolver, level it at him, and order him to put his hands on the car. He does and I turn and order the other one, who is still at the front of the car, to get down on the ground. He complies immediately. Suddenly the talker shouts, "No!" turns, and runs into the ditch.

Now I have two suspects – one on the ground and the other running – and I want both of them. If I am to get both of them, I have to stop the one who is running. What would make him stop? Maybe if he hears a bullet whiz by him, he'll stop, so I decide to fire a warning shot. It doesn't work – he keeps going. Now what to do? I really want to arrest both of them, but I see now that might not be possible.

I decide that if I can arrest only one, I want the one who is running. So I start running after him down into the ditch. At the bottom of the ditch in the high weeds I step into a hole, fall, and hit the ground so hard I lose my sunglasses. My pistol, still in my hand, goes off. I jump up and see the talker on his back on the others side of the fence, not moving. Instant terror goes through me – I'm afraid I accidentally shot him when I fell and the gun went off.

As I move toward him, I see he is starting to move and isn't bleeding. The sound of the gun going off apparently scared him and he jumped over the fence head first and was stunned when he hit the ground. The other guy is still lying on the ground in front of the car. I order him to come down and I handcuff him to the fence. Then I turn my attention back to the talker who is now sitting up. I point the gun at him and order him to lie face down.

He says, "Go ahead and shoot me – I don't care." (If he had ever seen any movies, he'd know the correct response is "Don't shoot – I give up." Instead, he says I'll have to shoot him, which, by now, is very tempting.)

He gets up and starts running again. Knowing that I really can't shoot him, I climb over the fence and start after him. All I really have to do is keep him in sight, since I have help coming. But I have a handicap due to the fact that I'm in full uniform carrying all my equipment, while he's in shorts.

We continue east for about a quarter mile, and then hit a gravel road, where he starts north. I have to settle for a pace I can maintain for a while, but I'm losing ground on him. I keep telling myself that all I have to do is keep him in sight. After another half-mile, I notice that I seem to be closing the distance between us – he's tiring and slowing down. In another quarter mile I catch up to him. He has pushed himself too hard and can't go any further, so just stops. I catch up, take him down, and handcuff him.

I'm still looking for my backup cars. It's a long walk back to my car as hot and tired as I am. Then I see a red car coming down the road. The driver stops and tells me he saw me chasing the suspect and came to see if he could help. I tell him I could sure use a ride back to my patrol car, and he's glad to oblige.

On the way back, the talker tells me if he could have made it to the creek he could have jumped in and gotten away from me by swimming. (Right, the creek is only two or three feet deep and I could walk along the bank faster than he could swim.) This kid isn't exactly the sharpest knife in the drawer.

When we arrive back at my patrol car, there are four troopers there, all standing and pointing their guns at the suspect I left handcuffed to the fence. They are shouting for him to put his hands up and he's trying to explain that he can't comply because he's handcuffed to the fence. My fellow troopers are really shocked when the red car pulls up and I get out with my prisoner. I tell them I got tired of waiting for them to show up, so I had to hitch a ride back.

Later on, I was able to determine that the talker had stolen the car at gun point in Nebraska and that the man with him was a hitchhiker he had picked up on the way to Iowa. The hitch hiker was released and told me he would never hitchhike again as long as he lives. The talker was returned to Nebraska where he was serving his time.

Not Your Typical Airline

I had earlier arrested a man wanted for burglary in Florida that I found sleeping in a car parked in an Interstate rest area. I booked him into the local jail and Florida authorities placed a hold on him for extradition.

About a week later I received a call from the jail that the suspect's extradition was being implemented and I was to pick him up and take him to the airport to meet a transport plane that would take him back to Florida. This procedure was a new one on me since usually extradited suspects were picked up by the officials from wherever they were going.

When I got to the airport with the suspect I observed that the plane on which he would be a passenger was not a commercial airliner, but a 24-passenger aircraft with no name on it. I escorted the prisoner to the plane as the door opened. Out came about twelve men shackled and handcuffed. Two guards came down first, then the prisoners, followed by two more guards who were also the pilots. They escorted the prisoners inside to use the restroom. The one female guard signed for my prisoner and we talked for a while. From the gun on her hip and her attitude toward the prisoners, it was obvious she was not your typical flight attendant.

She explained that her company contracted to transport prisoners all over the country. The aircraft had eye bolts in the floor and the prisoners were attached to these at all times while in flight. The guards and pilots were all armed. She was one of two who worked the cabin security while in flight as well as handling any female prisoners.

As the group of prisoners was being loaded back on the plane, one of them said, "I only waived extradition because they said I would fly back. I expected a commercial airline – not this." I watched until my prisoner was shackled and handcuffed, then led on board the plane.

Walking back to my car, I agreed that I would not want to fly that airline.

How Dumb Can They Get?

I was working traffic control during a winter storm on Interstate 80. The zero-degree temperature and 20-mile-per-hour wind created a wind chill factor 25 below zero. The wind was blowing the snow across the highway, greatly reducing visibility. There was a pile-up of semis that had completely blocked the road, trapping any additional cars that drove up to the wreck in the blinding storm.

We were attempting to direct traffic away from the wreck by sending drivers off the Interstate at the exit before the mess. We had two patrol cars blocking the roadway and we were taking turns being out of the car because of the harsh conditions. Down the road at the scene of the pile-up, officers were getting victims out of the wrecked vehicles and turning other vehicles around that had driven up to the site, heading them back toward us. As those vehicles approached, we would move a patrol car, so they could get by the roadblock and onto the exit ramp.

Any car approaching would see a patrol car being moved and a car going the wrong way, being let out and sent up the exit ramp. Invariably, someone would try to drive through the opening in the roadblock and head toward the pile-up. One of the other troopers finally asked, "How dumb can these people get?"

I responded, "That is a trick question, as it appears there is no limit."

It is an old joke: "Do you know the difference between genius and stupidity?"

ANSWER: There is a limit to genius.

Another one: "Do you know the difference between ignorance and stupidity?"

ANSWER: I don't know and I don't care.

How Did They Do That?

While working the night shift I met an oncoming car that failed to dim its headlights. I flashed my lights at it, but it still didn't dim the headlights. After passing him, I turned around in pursuit and as I overtook the car I noticed two odd things. First, there was a motorcycle hanging out of the trunk. Second, the license plate on the back of the car was bug spattered. You don't see many bug spattered license plates on the **back** of a car – you just don't back up that fast. A check showed the license plate did not belong on that car. Okay. I called in my location and asked for backup before I stopped the car.

Once I had pulled the car over, I approached with caution since I couldn't see into the car from the back because the trunk lid was up due to the motorcycle. There were three people in the car – two men and a woman – all in the front seat. I asked for license and registration. The driver had a license but no registration.

My backup had arrived so I asked them to exit the vehicle. As the driver got out, I spotted a gun on the seat. I took the gun and we handcuffed and searched them. No more weapons were found. By using a mirror, we were able to get the license plate number off the motorcycle. It was registered to a Des Moines man, so I called dispatch and asked them to call the owner and see if he knew the whereabouts of his motorcycle. In a few minutes, dispatch called and told us the man was upset at being bothered and that of course he knew where his motorcycle was – it was in his garage. I said, "Just ask him to go look as a favor to us."

He agreed, with some grumbling, to go look. One minute later, he was on the phone, "It's gone; it's gone."

I said, "We know that."

The car with the motorcycle still in the trunk was towed to a local garage and the three thieves were booked. The following day I got a call from the tow service. They said they didn't see how those three thieves got the motorcycle into the trunk of that car. It took three garage workers using a hoist to get it out.

Honor Among Thieves?

Despite what you see on television and at the movies this does not exist.

Case in point. At he beginning of the shift I stop a car for speeding, expired registration, no seat belt and a suspended license. The car smells like marijuana.

I ask, "Do you have any drugs in the car?" And I get my favorite answer, "Well, not that I am aware of".

Translation "Yes, but I am trying to lay a defense when you find the drugs". My next question, "Then you won't mind if I check would you?" "Well I guess not."

And of course I find Meth and Marijuana.

He says, "Look I am on parole can we make a deal? I can give you my supplier".

I call the Narcotics guys; they come out and talk to him.

The Narcs think it is worthwhile so we have him set up a buy. The supplier will bring it over so I wait and stop him on his way over. Sure enough he has more drugs. Same deal he is on probation, he will give up his supplier who is the girl he lives with.

Same set up she brings them I stop her, she decides to run and a short chase ensues in which she throws a paper sack of drugs out. We recover them.

Same deal she is on parole. She will set up her supplier her brother. The Narcs do want him they have been working on him but having no luck. So here we go again. I am beginning to think I just want to take someone to Jail and go home.

Turns out he is not willing to give up his suppliers as we are getting well up the food chain so he goes to Jail and I finally get to go home. The upside, the Narcs have to do most of the paperwork.

High Speed Pursuit

While patrolling Interstate 80 one day I attempted to stop a driver for speeding and not wearing a seat belt. I ran a check on the license plate and was told it was a stolen car. The driver took off and a high-speed chase resulted. However, this chase ended in a most unusual way.

When the driver realized he couldn't outrun me on the interstate highway, he exited and took a gravel road. About a half-mile down this road was a set of raised railroad tracks where all the locals knew to slow down before crossing. This man didn't know that and when he hit those tracks, he was tossed upwards and cracked his head on the car roof, knocking him out cold.

The car continued down into the ditch before rolling to a stop. I had just finished cuffing him, when he started to regain consciousness. Had he been wearing his seat belt, he might have escaped . . . or at least been spared a bad headache.

Hell Hath No Furry

I had received a report of a man walking down the center line on Interstate 80 near Altoona. When I arrived I saw a man staggering down the shoulder.

He was obviously drunk. When I talked to him I learn he and his wife had been traveling from Utah to Illinois for a family reunion. She was driving and he was drinking. An argument started and he told his wife just pull over and let me out. She did and drove off leaving him alongside the road miles from anywhere.

I arrested him for public intoxication and booked him at the Polk County Jail.

We all had a good laugh about her driving off and leaving him. I went back to patrol. About an hour later I got a message to call the Jail.

The jailer answered the phone and when he stopped laughing he told me the rest of the story. Down the road a few miles his wife realized he had all the money. She came back and when she failed to find him she called the Sheriffs Office and was told he was in jail. She went to the jail and told them her story.

They told her if he would sign a release for the money to her she could then post his bond and they could be on their way.

The husband was brought down signed the release of the money.

She took the money turned and left the jail and went on to the reunion or home leaving him in jail and with no money.

The Entertainer's Crew and the Carnies

Night shift at the Iowa State Fair is always interesting with the drunks, fights, crowds, con artists, and thieves, not to mention the clothing some people wear to the fair. On this night about midnight, the big show had been over for a while, the crowds had thinned out, and some of the vendors had started to close. I got a call there was trouble at the east end of the grandstand, where the carnival is located. No need to tell the other troopers – I knew they'd be on the way.

When I got there, I found two groups facing off and hurling insults back and forth. I talked to both sides to find out the problem. The loading dock for the grandstand stage is located next to the carnival. So, when the Stage shows trucks had backed in to unload the band's equipment and set up for the show, the drivers had to sleep in their sleeper cabs of their trucks. Since it was August in Iowa, they had left their trucks running so the air conditioners would keep them cool. They would be driving that night, getting the equipment to the next town. As the trucks idled, their fumes drifted into the carnival area. Why the carnival workers hadn't complained earlier I don't know, but now they were confronting the loaders and drivers as they were preparing to leave.

I have learned the best way to get people to listen when they have been yelling is to speak in a voice just loud enough to force them to listen closely to hear you. After giving each side their say, I explained that I was not wearing a striped shirt or a robe, and that I am not a referee or judge, and am only interested in keeping the peace – and this is how I intended to do that. I told them if there were any more problems I would arrest all involved. Any carnival workers I arrested would be barred from returning to the fair, which meant the carnival would replace them and they would have no ride to the next stop. The show people liked this, but I told them that any from their group that I arrested would go to jail. Unfortunately, the booking process at the fair, followed by the wait for transfer to the jail, re-booking at the jail, and getting a bond posted would not be finished until long after the sun was up. Since the trucks had to make the next show, they would leave long before the processing was done, leaving them trying to figure out how to get to the next stop – if they still had a job.

I then said, "Ladies and gentlemen, if you do not believe me, just try me as I'll be here all night! I suggest you return to your work – Now!" An hour later, after no further incidents, I saw the trucks leave. Then it was time to check the parking lots for cars that had been reported stolen by owners who had simply forgotten where they parked them. Once the lots cleared out, they were easy to find.

Rocky Marciano
(World Champ Boxer)

On August 30th, 1969 we received a report from some people living south of the Newton Airport that they had heard an airplane flying low over their house sounding like it was having engine trouble. They thought it might have crashed.

I was at the Post #1 office in Des Moines with a Sergeant, who decided to ride along with me when I went to check it out. We were able to locate the witnesses at their house south of the Airport. They told us they had heard the plane go over their house, much lower than other planes, and then the engine noise just stopped. They also thought they'd heard a crash in the area between their house and the airport less than a mile away.

The area between their house and the airport was all farm ground (no roads). It was night and it was foggy. I found an entrance to a field and drove in trying to follow the dirt paths in the general direction of the airport. It was rough going with the patrol car bouncing along through the holes and ruts.

I was very glad that I had replaced the bulb in my spotlight with a 100,000 candlepower aircraft landing light.

Finally, after bouncing around back and forth around the fields, I picked up something white sticking up in some trees. It was across a field without even a cow path across it. As I started driving across the field, Sgt. Moore said, "What are you doing?"

"Going over there," I replied.

It was a rough ride with the car frame occasionally bottoming out on the ground, but we made it and it was the crashed airplane. I was relieved since I was sure Sgt. would otherwise have chewed me out good for taking the patrol car across that rough field. We found three bodies in the aircraft wreckage.

The fire department was on the scene by then, but didn't want to try to bring fire trucks or an ambulance across that field for fear of getting stuck. They did have an old Dodge Power Wagon 4-wheel drive "attack truck" with high ground clearance that got to us. That was how we got the medical examiner to the crash site and the bodies transported out to the hearse.

When we checked the bodies for identification, we found one of the men was Rocky Marciano, former boxing world heavyweight champion during the 1950s. Frankie Farrell was the other passenger. The pilot had no instrument rating and should not have been flying in that weather. Rocky had a money clip in his pocket with a two carat diamond in it and inscribed "To the Rock" and holding $5010.00 in cash.

The Great Flood of 1993

The spring of 1993 was the Great Flood of Iowa. Experts said a flood of this size happened every 500 or 1,000 years, depending on to whom you listened. The Des Moines Water Works was flooded, leaving the city and many of its suburbs without any water supply. The downtown area flooded and most of the power was out.

The Patrol was challenged to keep up with routing traffic away from flooded roads that had to be closed on short notice. There was also a lot of work rescuing people who drove into places where water was over the road, stalling their vehicles. One man went to his house to remove some of their belongings before the flood hit and decided to drink the beer in the refrigerator before he left so it would not go to waste. He passed out and when he woke up, his house was surrounded by water and we had to send a boat to get him out.

While it was a bad time for many people, it was also heartwarming to see people work together and observe the aid that came in from all over the country. Our home was supplied by a well, so we were able to offer people water, laundry, and shower facilities.

When the Raccoon River just west of Des Moines flooded its banks and covered Interstate 80 in that area, the highway had to be closed and traffic detoured. The Iowa D.O.T. sent all westbound traffic south at the Waukee exit to Booneville and then west to Highway F-90 to get back onto I-80, with the reverse for eastbound. When I came on duty and went to the Waukee exit, traffic was backed up for two miles on I-80. The trucks created a bottleneck at Booneville trying to turn the corner and ascend a long, steep hill. I checked and Highway #6 was still open, so I told the troopers to send the trucks north to Highway #6 and the cars to the south. I drove to F-90 and did the same thing, but sent the trucks back to exit 100 to get onto Highway #6, which cleared that backup as well. I had contacted Dallas County Sheriff, and Adel and Waukee Police Departments to expect the trucks.

About two hours after we had cleared up the backlogs, the district engineer for the D.O.T. arrived. He told me that Highway #6 was not the "official detour" and that ALL traffic had to go through Booneville. I told him that I was sorry I did not realize that and I would correct the situation. I thanked him for stopping by and clearing everything up for us, then escorted him back to his pickup truck. After he left, I walked back to the intersection where one of my troopers asked, "Well, what do we do now, Sarge?"

I said, "We keep doing what is working. If he comes back, I'll apologize for my confusion." He did not come back.

We were kept very busy as the water level continued to rise and we had to close more roads and figure out detours. We had been loaned some people from the Iowa National Guard Military Police, so after we got a road closed and barricaded, I would post them to keep people from driving around the barricades. However, their commander didn't want them to be "out front" where people could talk to them (I don't know why), but their presence kept the people who would have driven around the barricades and into water from doing so. Yes, there *were* people who tried to do that.

While we were trying to close Interstate 35, I got a call from the Emergency Operations Center (EOC) at Camp Dodge. This was a bunch of management people from various agencies sitting in an underground bunker drinking coffee and eating donuts attempting to run the operation with no real idea of what was going on outside the bunker. Relaying the message, my dispatcher informed me that, "E.O.C. is checking to see if you have a trooper who could go to the University Avenue D.O.T. shop and pick up a man and take him out to see if the water is over Highway Six." Of course, my first inclination was to tell them, "Just tell him to get his lazy butt out in one of those orange trucks and drive himself out there. We are busy!" However, I waited a few seconds and said simply, "Negative. We are all busy."

Later, Lt, who had been the Patrol's representative at the E.O.C., contacted me and apologized for that request. He said there was no way he could tell them to not ask. He told me he knew what I must have thought and thanked me for not saying it. I did find one way to stop drivers from driving around the cones we placed on blocked exit ramps. I used the "POLICE LINE DO NOT CROSS" ribbon. They might move the cones, drive around them, or, in some cases, run over them if no one was there, but for some reason they would not cross that tape.

The Leg

It was a hot summer day at Saylorville Lake. I answered a radio call of a serious personal injury traffic accident a half-mile west of the Mile-Long Bridge. A car had sideswiped a man and his wife on a motorcycle. They each had their left leg torn off in the accident. The police and fire rescue crews did a great job in a quick response and getting them to the hospital alive. As it turned out, however, the victims were devout Christian Science followers and refused blood transfusions and died at the hospital.

At the accident scene, once the ambulance left for the hospital, I completed my measurements and investigation. We decided to go to the Polk City Police/Fire Station to complete the paperwork in the cool air conditioning. The cause of the accident was that the driver of the car was distracted watching the boats on the lake and crossed the center line, striking the motorcycle.

As I was finishing my paperwork and preparing to leave for the hospital, the ambulance returned and an embarrassed-looking fire chief approached me. He explained that when they got back to the fire house and started cleaning the ambulance, they found one of the legs we had put in a plastic bag under one of the seats. (This was in the days before they reattached severed limbs, and these had been torn off, not cut.)

I told him I was ready to go to the hospital and would deliver it. He handed me the plastic bag containing the leg. The bag was tied with a knot at the top. When I got to the hospital, I grabbed my equipment and the plastic bag by the knot and headed in the Emergency Entrance door. As I was going in, two elderly ladies were coming out. At that instant, the bottom of the plastic bag gave way, spilling the severed leg onto the floor.

The ladies stopped, took one look at the mess (one said "Oh, my god!), and took off at what I thought was an amazing speed for their age. I picked up the leg and tried to cover it with the bag as best I could and went in, trying to find someone in the ER to give it to. Handling it was like I was holding a live snake and trying to pass it on. No one would take it. A couple ran away as they saw me walking toward them. I must admit that I may have had just a little fun with it until I finally got a sheet and wrapped it up. I put it in an empty examination room before the nurse in charge arrived. I was sure she would not be scared (or would have seen the humor).

Post Script: The driver of the car was found to be the total cause of the accident and completely liable, but he had no insurance, no job, and no assets. The couple on the motorcycle had three young children. I was asked to testify in court twice as they tried to find someone to sue. First, it was the Corps of Engineers for an alleged bridge defect. But that was thrown out after I testified that the accident occurred a half-mile from the bridge. Then they tried to sue the insurance company of the previous owner of the car, as it had been less than 30 days since the car had been sold, but that was also denied.

The Law of Salvage

The first arrest I made that wasn't for a traffic offense was a very unusual one.

I was still in my training period and had my training officer in the car. I had stopped for a motorist assist. The car was out of gas, so I took the driver to a gas station and we were returning to his car.

As we got close I noticed the hood on his car was up – it had been closed when we left. I then observed a man walking up the road carrying a car battery. I stopped him and asked where he had gotten the battery.

He said that he had found it in that abandoned car. I was surprised that in the short amount of time that we had been gone that he had been able to get to the car and remove the battery. My training officer informed me that this individual came from a family who had a lot of experience removing car parts quickly. They felt that the law of salvage on the high seas also applied to highways. If you left your car along the road, it was fair game to them.

Turkeys on the Road

It was a nice fall day. I was working the day shift when the call came, a report of "a truck load of live turkeys overturned in the median on Interstate 35." I responded, "In route. Start some more cars." I could picture turkeys flying across the north and southbound lanes of the interstate and cars hitting them or going into the ditch to avoid the turkeys as they rushed to escape.

When I got there, I was surprised to find that the turkeys were out, but not flying off. They were trying to get back into their cages. I guess that was the only life they knew and they were afraid to leave it for the unknown. They didn't know they were on the way to be processed for Thanksgiving.

That gave me a new understanding of why abused women and children don't leave their abusers. I also learned that we should not expect people or animals to do what we would necessarily do in any situation. Expect the worst and hope for the best in people.

Three at a Time

Early one morning while working the Iowa State Fair I checked the carnival overflow parking lot for any vehicles that had not been there the last time I checked. The carnival workers overflow lot is where the late-coming employees or new hires park. In the past, I had recovered many stolen vehicles there, usually with the thief sleeping in it.

This time I saw three motorcycles parked outside an open semi-trailer and three men sleeping inside. I ran a check on the license plates. No stolen report, but two of the license plates were registered to Hondas and these three were all Harley Davidsons. I checked and the threesome was still sleeping. I quietly recorded the vehicle identification number from each motorcycle. One of them had obviously been altered, but only one number was stamped over into an "8" so it had to be a 3, 6, or 9. When I checked on the numbers, they were all stolen.

I called for backup.

Now the problem was that I did not actually see the three men with those stolen motorcycles, so they could just say, "I don't know where they came from." When my backup arrived, I had them wait out of sight around the corner of the trailer. I then woke the three men and told them there was no motorcycle parking in this lot and if these were their bikes, they needed to move them. They immediately headed for the bikes with keys in hand.

THANK YOU!

I said, "Wait!" and called the troopers from around the corner, then continued, "Oh, did I mention they are stolen bikes and you are now under arrest?"

The motorcycles had been stolen from Hutchinson, Kansas, and a friend of mine was a Kansas trooper living there, so I called him. I told him about the arrest and described the motorcycle gang colors they were wearing. They were well known to him. In fact, he and the Hutchinson police had wanted to raid the gang's clubhouse because they were drug dealers. So this was a perfect situation to get a search warrant. He asked if I could delay their phone call. I told him that was no problem since they would have to wait until they were transferred to the city jail before they could get a phone call. I told him I would call one of my Vehicle Theft guys to come here to the fairgrounds to interview them first and he lived an hour away and may have some trouble with traffic. I asked him to call me when they had their warrant and were ready to go in, then I'd make sure they did get their phone call shortly after the police entered the gang's clubhouse. I said, "You can answer the phone and tell him hello for me."

They sent ten to prison and the gang broke up shortly thereafter.

4 VEHICLE ARRESTS AT FAIR

By STEVEN KLAUS
Register Assistant State Editor

State troopers arrested three persons last weekend on the grounds of the Iowa State Fair for driving motorcycles that were either stolen or had altered identification numbers.

A fourth man was arrested Tuesday for possession of a stolen car.

The motorcyclists arrested are J. D. Dodds, 25; Dodds' half-brother, Cecil E. Raines, 23; and Paul R. Smith, 24, all of Topeka, Kan. Dodds and Raines are charged with second-degree theft and possession of a vehicle with altered serial numbers. Smith was charged with possession of a vehicle with altered serial numbers. Troopers seized the three motorcycles.

Lt. Loren Dykeman said the three men, who were seeking employment at the fair, were arrested after Trooper Charles Black checked the license plates on the motorcycles, learned that two of them were stolen Aug. 12 in Topeka, Kan., and called in a state vehicle theft officer.

Dodds and Raines were being held in the Polk County Jail Tuesday in lieu of $5,100 bond each. Dykeman said Smith was released after posting bond.

Robert B. Taylor, 22, of Long Beach, Calif., was arrested Tuesday for larceny of a motor vehicle and possession of a controlled substance. Dykeman said Taylor was arrested after Sgt. Dewey Jontz checked the license plates on the 1971 Dodge he was driving, discovered it was stolen Aug. 1 in Long Beach, and summoned a vehicle theft officer.

With the 3 Stolen Motorcycles

A Car Load

I was working the evening shift. It was after dark when I stopped at a four ways stop I glanced over at the convenience store on the corner. The store had two sides that were lighted (one the Front) and two that were dark.

I saw that three men were urinating on the lighted side. I swung around and pulled in behind their car, blocking it. There were two men inside the car.

An off duty Deputy, who was working in the convenience store, saw me pull in and he came over to see what was happening.

As I talked to the men in the car I could determine they were drunk. None of them had driver's licenses and when I ran checks on the group, four of them had outstanding warrants.

The deputy called for the Sheriff's car assigned to this area on his walkie-talkie and a deputy and the shift Supervisor drove over. I arrested all five men for various combinations of public intoxication, public urination and outstanding warrants.

I loaded two into my car, the deputy took two, and the shift supervisor put the last one in his car.

My dispatcher didn't know that the deputy and his supervisor were there with me when I called in to say, "In route to the jail with five."

There was a delay in reply and then he asked"

Checking, with five?"

I responded, "10-4".

It's not a good idea for one trooper to try to handle five suspects. First of all he's badly outnumbered, secondly a single trooper does not usually carry five pairs of handcuffs, and finally there's the problem of fitting five grown men into three seats.

When I called to tell the dispatcher that I would be out of contact while I was at the jail, he asked me to call him when I was not busy.

When I did finally call him, he just wanted to know how I got five men in my car. He never doubted that I had done it. He just wanted to know how.

Aliens Have Put a Radio in my Head

When the Iowa State Patrol set up its new 1-800 hotline to be manned 24-7, it rang in to the post office, but they hadn't set up anyone to answer it. So, for a few months during the 11 PM. to 7 AM. shift, a road trooper had to be in the office to answer the phone. Most nights it was really boring. You had to make your own entertainment – read books, listen to the radio . . . pace. When there was a true emergency like a winter storm where more help was needed on the road, you were frustrated because you were stuck in the post office with the phone.

One boring night the phone rang. I answered, "Emergency Line. Trooper Black."

The voice on the other end said, "Aliens have put a radio in my head and I can hear them talking to me."

Okay, now what do I say – or do?

I replied, "Have you contacted the local police?"

"Yes, I have contacted the police, sheriff, the FBI, and the CIA."

"And what did they tell you?"

"They took me to a hospital, but after a few days they released me."

I asked him to hold the line for a minute and called the local police department. They informed me that, yes, they knew him. In fact, they had committed him twice resulting for mental health evaluations, but the judge released him both times claiming he did not present a danger to himself or others. After that, they just told the caller not to listen to the voices when he continued to call. I had a hunch we were going to hear from him again and again, so it was time to try a new approach.

Switching the line back to the caller I said, "Have you tried lining your hat with tin foil?"

"No. I haven't – why?" he asked

I explained, "The tin foil blocks radio signals. But be sure it is the shiny side facing up or out."

"But what about when I'm in my house when I sleep?"

"Radio signals come in through the windows so if you do the same thing with putting tin foil on the windows, it will block the signals as well."

The caller thanked me and hung up.

A week later I got a call from the local police asking if I would stop by. When I got there they wanted to know what I told the guy. They had observed his windows covered with tin foil and could also see the foil under his hat. He told them that I had fixed the problem for him.

The good news is he stopped calling in.

Ambulance/Hearse

In the late 1960s when I was a new patrolman, there were no ambulance crews, no Emergency Medical Technicians and no First Responders. When we handled a serious crash with injuries and called for an ambulance, we'd get the hearse from one of the local funeral homes. It came with a driver and a stretcher. They took out the coffin and put in a stretcher.

Patrol officers were trained in first aid, so we applied bandages and set splints while we waited for the ambulance. We placed the injured victims onto stretchers and loaded them in the back of the hearse, which then took off for the nearest hospital. Our dispatcher notified the hospital that an ambulance was on its way so they could have a doctor waiting. I often wondered if we loaded an unconscious person and he woke up alone in the back of that moving hearse and looked around, what he might think. It would scare the devil out of me.

In Des Moines, the Yellow Cab Company did have an actual ambulance. It was a modified hearse (of course) with a red light and siren, and kept at the company's Des Moines maintenance garage. As a result, the driver was the mechanic who serviced the cabs. On one occasion when the Yellow Cab ambulance showed up, the driver had made an attempt to clean up by washing his hands, but his arms and wrists were covered with grease.

He opened the back door of the hearse and said, "Oh, no. I forgot the stretcher." So, we made a bed out of blankets and he took off for the hospital.

I always felt that if the victims survived all of that and got to the hospital alive, they had a good chance of making it.

A Good Way to Start the Day?

I had started the early day shift at 6 AM. As usual, I drove through the Interstate rest area and called dispatch to check license plates on the cars parked there for any warrants. I have discovered several stolen cars or wanted people doing this.

While I was waiting for results from dispatch, one of the cars I had checked, a Mustang, pulled out. As it was leaving the rest area, I got the report that it was a stolen car. I started after it on westbound Interstate 80.

When I tried to stop the Mustang, it took off. While in pursuit I called for someone ahead to get ready to help. I was told the nearest car was 80 miles ahead. I was running wide open at about 110 miles per hour (slowest car I ever had) with lights flashing and siren blaring, passing the few cars on the road that early, but I was slowly losing ground on the Mustang.

Suddenly I spotted smoke and fire coming from the Mustang. My first thought was it had blown an engine. I was wrong – the Mustang kept going, though now a little slower. I started closing the gap. Later I learned that he had thrown a tread on a steel belted radial tire and the fire was from the steel belt hitting the concrete pavement. The tire still held air.

As I got closer, the driver of the Mustang decided to try an old trick. As he approached an exit ramp, he waited until the last second to swerve off. There are two problems with this strategy for trying to escape:

One:I am far enough behind him to be able to make the exit; and

Two:He is too close to the ramp and ends up in the grass between the ramp and highway, though he continues on at a high rate of speed in the ditch. I am on the exit ramp running parallel to him.

Now he has a third problem: There is a sharp rise at the end of the ditch where the crossroad goes up to pass over the Interstate.

The Mustang hit the rise, then went airborne with the front end pointing skyward. It passed over the crossroad (I swear) high enough to clear the road *and* a semi - had one been there. The car continued on and landed on its rear end, then turned onto its side. I was sure the driver must be dead or at least seriously injured.

To my surprise, he climbed out the car window and started to run. I pursued on foot. He lost a shoe in the crash and I was able to catch him, knock him to the ground, and get him cuffed. As I escorted him to my patrol car, I noticed a lady who had parked her car behind mine. She yelled at the driver of the Mustang, "You almost killed me when you cut me off!" After calming her down, I loaded the prisoner into my car and transported him to jail.

Later, my dispatcher called and told me that the Kansas City Police Department reported that the driver of the Mustang had murdered the owner of the car in order to get it. He was also an escapee from a Texas prison. When a tow truck righted the Mustang, we found his shoe and a pistol in the car. He had the gun on the seat beside him but lost it when he hit the embankment. The Kansas City PD filed extradition papers on the suspect and Texas prison officials sent someone to Iowa to question the suspect about how he escaped, because they had no idea how he did it.

The county jail I booked the suspect into found out what a "Houdini" he was. First, he managed to remove a bolt from a toilet and used it to cut into the ceiling and get into the overhead, though there was no escape from up there. So the jailers removed him to a new cell and decided to chain him to the bed. By the time they got outside, the suspect was at the window, yelling at them, "I am free of the chains." Finally, they called in one of the senior deputies to chain him again. This time the restraints held.

Later that afternoon the suspect complained to jailers of pain and soreness, so they took him to the local doctor in leg shackles and handcuffs. The prisoner told the doctor that he needed strong prescription medication in large quantities. He named the drugs and dosages. The doctor, who had been treating prisoners for many years replied, "I think Tylenol will take care of it."

I heard the suspect eventually ended up at one of Missouri's maximum security prisons.

Sgt. Charles A Black

Texas fugitive nabbed

DeSOTO — An 18-year-old escapee from a Texas state penitentiary was apprehended near here after a high speed chase through Dallas County Monday morning.

Iowa State Patrol Trooper Charles Black said a routine license check at the Waukee area rest stop on Interstate 80 at about 6:15 a.m. resulted in the arrest of Troy L. Shaffer. Shaffer escaped Friday from the Texas penitentiary at Austin, where he was serving time for burglary. Black said the license check revealed the car was stolen in Kansas City early Monday morning.

Shaffer led Black on a high speed chase, with speeds reaching 115 miles per hour, before he lost control of the stolen car on the Dallas County F90 exit ramp. Black said the car traveled from the ramp to the median dividing it from the interstate, hit an embankment and then vaulted airborne across Dallas County F90 before landing on its top. Shaffer began to run from the scene and was arrested a short distance from the crash site. Shaffer suffered only minor bruises and abrasians in the crash.

Shaffer was charged with failure to maintain control of his vehicle, attempting to ellude a police officer, speeding and second degree theft.

Black said Shaffer's arrest also clears up three early Monday morning burglaries in Warren County, where possible charges are also pending. Shaffer also is wanted in Missouri in connection with the car theft. He is being held in the Dallas County Jail at Adel, pending extradition by Texas authorities.

Backseat Fatality

I was called to the scene of a tragic fatal car accident. Two teen-age drivers had hit head-on at the crest of a hill on a gravel road. The cars ended up in ditches on opposite sides of the road. When I arrived, it was clear that both drivers were deceased, but it was still necessary to call the local medical examiner, who, at that time, was an elderly man with failing eyesight.

He did fine in the autopsy room where his eyes had time to adjust to the light. He usually assigned his assistant to handle all the outdoor calls, but he was not available that day. So, the doctor had his nurse drive him out to the scene.

Knowing he would have trouble getting to the first wrecked car, I helped him. The car was tipped at an angle and the driver was lying in the seat with his head against the door. I knew if I opened that door, the body would slide out in the doctor's lap, so I opened the back door so the doctor could reach over the front seat to check him. I didn't think about the doctor's eyesight and that he would be in the sun and the body in the shade.

The doctor leaned in through the back door, felt around the back seat area, stepped back and proclaimed: "Yes, he is dead."

I saw no reason to question his statement and embarrass him the body was definitely dead and I was sure the backseat was also.

Best Comebacks

Here are some of the best comebacks I've heard in exchanges between troopers and the public:

Driver: "Do you know who my father is?"
Trooper: "Sorry, I can't help you there."
Driver: "Do you know who I am?"
Trooper: "Sorry, but maybe someone at the jail will."
Driver (driving by the scene of a bad crash asks): "Have an accident?"
Trooper: "No, thanks. Already got one."
Driver: "I always heard troopers do not give tickets to pretty girls."
Trooper: "That's right. Sign here, please."

A main approaches two troopers having lunch and asks: "Do you want my opinion on the seat belt law?"

Trooper: "No, but thank you for offering
Driver: I guess you have to make your quota of tickets?
Trooper: Yes sir, two more and I get a toaster oven.

The Boy Scout and the Drunk Driver

I was the leader of a Boy Scout troop for several years and had an unusual incident occur one night coming home from a scout meeting. It had been a Boy Scout Court of Honor, so I had my family and some scouts in the car. As we followed another car down the road, the man behind the wheel was doing a very bad job of driving. It quickly became apparent that he was drunk.

I decided I was not going to try to stop him with my family in my personal car. About a mile from my home he pulled into a church parking lot. I continued home as quickly as I could, grabbed my gun belt, jumped into my patrol car, told my wife to take the kids home and drove back to that church lot. Luck was with me – he was still there. I arrested him and took him to jail for testing and booking. All this time I was in my Boy Scout uniform.

The next morning he tried to explain to the judge that he was not drunk, and that some Boy Scout had arrested him.

Death Notifications

One of the worst parts of my job as a trooper was to notify families of the death of a loved one. You are going to a home or work place to tell someone you don't know that they have lost someone they love.

The only hard rule is to never do this alone. I tried to locate another family member, friend, or minister. When this was not possible, I always took another trooper or local officer. Ideally, I always knocked on the door and make sure it was the right person. The reactions were as varied as there are people.

In one case I went to the door and knocked. A lady opened the door, looked at me and said, "No, no, no," then slammed the door.

In another incident, when I told the lady there had been an accident and her husband had been killed, she started yelling, "You are lying! You are lying! Why are you lying to me?"

One lady attacked me, hitting me in the chest and screaming.

Another lady just stood up and walked around the room saying, "No," over and over.

However one lady when I told her that her husband had been killed in a traffic accident just replied "Good". And then just shut the door.

There is no easy way to do it and no way that is right in every case. I always left with an empty feeling inside and wondered how I could have made it easier for them.

Grill Donor Program

The Iowa State Patrol has just started it grill donor program. This program allows troopers who have chrome grills in their patrol cars to donate those grill to headquarters personnel who have black grills in their new unmarked cars. It has always been the Troopers way to help out those in need. Can you imagine the suffering and shame our leaders must be forced to endure by not having a shiny chrome grill in their new cars. The stigma attached to not having a chrome grill cannot be allowed to continue.

With this worthwhile program in mind we are trying to come up with a slogan for this program please, submit you suggestions.

Here are some suggestions:

1. Don't be a pill, give up your grill
2. Don't keep it away, brighten up their day.
3. There is no need to cry and moan, I will give you my grill of chrome.
4. If you will just chill, I will give you my grill.

Iowa Jam

For a few years, the grandstand at the Iowa State Fairgrounds hosted the "Iowa Jam" – concerts of hard rock bands. Young people traveled from all over to attend. The Fair Office opened the Fairgrounds Campground the night before the events. It became a drunken mess.

The next morning, a group of us troopers were assigned to work the day-long event. We arrived before the 10 AM show time, just as people were coming down the hill from the campground to the grandstand. It was obvious that some were very drunk. Two troopers were assigned to the entrance to the show, along with parents looking for runaways. Cans or glass bottles were prohibited, so many of the campers had purchased gallons of milk in plastic jugs from local stores. After pouring out the milk, they filled the jugs with beer. I'm sure that milk-flavored beer at 80 degrees is really bad, but as long as it was beer, they didn't care.

We arrested those who were too drunk to make it safely down the hill. What a fun experience they had: Drive from Minnesota to Des Moines, pay $50 for a show ticket, get drunk and arrested, miss the show, post a $125-bond to get out of jail. Fun, fun, fun.

After the show started, our work continued. We circled the crowd, which was packed tight, and arrested the ones so drunk they either staggered out or were thrown out by the rest of the crowd. We were like wolves circling the herd, picking off the ones unable to take care of themselves or stay with the protective mob. Instead of eating them, we put them in a safe place to sleep it off.

Jeep Help?

In the 1960s we had "help" patrolling the highways during the summer holiday weekends. The Iowa National Guard Military Police came out in their Jeeps and we gave them license plates that said: "Auxiliary Highway Patrol" which they installed on each vehicle. I have no idea who thought this was a good idea,

Back then, the speed limits were 70 MPH on the two-lane highways and 75 MPH on the Interstates. Now picture this: a Jeep with a top speed of about 45 MPH driving down the highway with miles of traffic behind it.

It's a wonder we didn't have some of the MPs killed or some major accidents caused by our "help."

We ended up having them park in the crossovers and observe traffic which they were very happy to do.

Pilot Stories

The Iowa State Patrol has an Air Wing. The trooper/pilots who fly the planes have very interesting stories to tell.

One of the best (or worst) is a trooper/pilot found a Bantam rooster somewhere and took it up in the aircraft with him. When he was at about 5,000 feet, he tossed it out of the aircraft. Since Bantam chickens can fly, that's exactly what it did. The rooster set his wing and just circled until he got to the ground. The trooper/pilot followed the rooster down observing that once on the ground it suffered from dizziness, taking two steps and falling over, followed by two more steps and falling, until the dizziness wore off. Another trooper/pilot, hearing this story, decided to try this for himself, so he found a chicken, went up, and threw it out. Unfortunately, he had a barnyard chicken and they can't fly.

It was common for trooper/pilots to work road patrol enforcement teamed with patrol cars on the ground, with the aircraft spotting violations and the patrol cars stopping the cars and issuing tickets or warnings. When it was time for a break, the trooper/pilot would often land close to the nearest patrol car which would pick him up, then return him to the aircraft after the break.

They often landed on dead-end gravel roads, at closed drive-in theaters, or in farmers' hayfield, anywhere that was handy. On a few occasions, this did not work out so well.

In one instance the aircraft was landed and left in a hayfield while the trooper/pilot went to lunch. Unknown to him, the farmer had put his pigs in that field. By the time they returned, the pigs had eaten the fabric off the bottom of the aircraft.

Another time a trooper/pilot landed in a field and went to lunch with some other troopers. The farmer's son had gotten a speeding ticket that morning. When the officers returned, they found the son had taken the tractor and plowed circles around the aircraft. The troopers had to push the aircraft by hand over the ruts to a place where the plane could take off.

Legal Intervention

It was a quiet summer day and I had been assigned to work one of the rural counties with the Interstate running through it. I was just exiting to a gas stations to get a cold drink. I got a call of a car driving off without paying for gas at that station and it had left northbound.

As I got to the stop sign the car came by and I pulled in behind it. Sometimes these are people who just forgot but sometimes more. There was one male in the car. I called in the license plate and dispatch confirmed it was a stolen car.

I switched on the top lights and the car took off at high speed. I called dispatch and advised them I was in pursuit and that I was switching to local law enforcement channel. I called to police in the next town and asked them to set up a road block. He was driving like a fool passing on top of hills at 100+.

The road block was getting set up when the stolen car turned off on a gravel road about a mile out of town and headed west. Since the car was stolen out of state I doubted he knew the roads. 2 miles ahead was a T intersection and I knew if he turned north the city police cars would set up a road there, but if the turned south we were going to have a long chase on the gravel roads.

When we approached the T intersection I saw him turn north but he was going to fast and spun out and ended up pointing south.

I decided it was time to end it now before someone got hurt. I rammed his car before he could get it going, right front corner to left front corner.

Not a lot of damage but it stunned him and by the time he recovered and tried to start his car I had his car door open grabbed two handfuls of hair and put him face down on the ground. Help arrived and I got him cuffed and booked. The Sgt came did an accident report. My car was still drivable all it looked like was I had pushed the front fenders and grill to the left.

I started back to the office to start the repair process.

As I passed through one of the small towns city officers saw me and I stopped. He wanted to know about the pursuit. We were talking in our cars just off the highway but out of sight when I heard a motorcycle coming fast. It passed by, I said "good by" and took off in pursuit. I was running over 110 and gaining on him when my hood opened. It did not come off it just laid over the windshield and smashed the top lights. It was blocking my view. There was a small gap between the hood and the dash in the center I could lean over and see through.

I pulled the car over to the shoulder and sat there for a few minutes then got out and looked at the hood. I grabbed the hood and pulled it back down. The problem was where it had hit the top lights. It had bent the up and it would not catch. I thought "well it is ruined anyway" so I climbed up on the hood and jump up and down on the end till it bent back enough to latch and ran a couple of bungee cords over it.

I wonder what people who drove by thought when they saw me jumping up and down on the hood of the patrol car.

I was not to far from home so I just radioed in that I would bring the car in the morning and went home.

I sure got some funny looks as drove the patrol car with the hood bent up and bungee cords across it in rush hour traffic the next morning.

I was given Kamikaze Award by Troopers at the post meeting

I Told Him Not to Ask

It is an old saying that a good attorney never asks a question in court he does not know the answer too.

This story will show that not all attorneys are good ones.

I am in court testifying on a third offense drunk driving case. Now by the rules of the court, the prosecution cannot bring up the fact that the d defendant has 2 prior convictions for drunk driving as it might prejudice the jury.

I have testified that the defendant was weaving down the road, smelled strongly of alcohol, failed all of the walk and balance tests and refused to take a breath test.

Now, it is the defense attorney's turn to cross- examine me. He goes over my testimony again trying to trip me up.

He comes to the refusal to give a breath test. The law regarding this is the implied consent law and there is a form I must fill out and a lot of information I must read to the drunk. He asked if I read it to him and I reply, "yes I did". He asked, "did he understand it". I answer, "yes I believe he did".

I can see the light up he thinks he has a handle to work on. He plans to try to show that if his client understood the form he could not have been very drunk. I don't think he sees where I am planning to go on this.

He asks "How are you so sure he understood the form?

I answer, "I am not sure I should answer that question".

He pulls himself up and says I have asked the question and you must answer it.

(O.K. butt head here comes your answer) I reply, "well as many times as he has been arrest and had it read to him he must understand it by now".

His face turns red and he turns to the judge shouting, "I object"!

The judge looks down and tells him, "Councilor it was your question and he told you not to ask it, over ruled, proceed".

The prosecuting attorney picks up his legal pad and holds it in front of his face to cover his laughing.

Now the defendants attorney has to ask me how many prior convictions he has on his record, because it sounded like more than two. So thanks to his attorney the jury is aware of his prior convictions.

But he is still not done doing damage to his clients case. I have explained the rest of the procedure and that when I finished it I returned his client to the booking area.

"And tell me trooper did you have any further conversation with my client after he was returned to the booking area?"

I have trouble not breaking into a big grin as I reply,

"Yes I did".

He asks, and what was that conversation about?

I answer, "I asked him, did you shit you pants"? And he said, (now I shift into the same ready to crying voice he used), "I'm sorry".

He objects and again the judge tells him, it was your question.

Post script. The drunk was convicted of third offense drunk driving and had to serve 30 days. The lawyer is still practicing law, he needs the practice!

The Iowa State Fair

The Iowa State Fair grounds are open all year round for different events besides the Fair.

They have their own police force but it is small and not able to handle the State air so now the Troopers come in to handle the fair. Now we send 40 troopers to work the fair but in the late 1960's and early

1970's it was very different.

You did not take your family to the Fair after dark.

The beer tents were packed and it was a drunken mess. We used to call it "Fighting and dancing nightly to the music of". Fights would start and just get bigger with groups roaming around fighting.

The problem was The Des Moines Police, Sheriff's office and the Patrol all had men there but when these mini –riots started no one was in charge and by the time we got organized it was out of control. This went on for several years and it looked like it would end the Fair.

Finally the governor asked the patrol chief how to save the fair. The Chief told him the Patrol would take over policing the Fair and we would send enough troopers in to do that.

We would be in charge.
We sent in enough men so that at night every time you turned around there was a trooper.

We would average 100 arrests per night and 130 on Friday and Saturday. We wanted to send a very clear message that the days drunken riots were over. It took a while and some people had to be arrested over and over but they got the word and the fair became a place you could take your family at night and feel safe.

During the first few years we would arrest them hold, them till we got a van load and send the down to the Police Department to book them in. We packed the vans I still remember a Des Moines officer telling me "I opened the door and they started coming out and they just kept coming". "Do you know how many there were in that van? 28 people!"

I told him I thought it was odd when the vans bumper drug going over the tracks of a small train that went around the fair grounds.

When we looked at our arrest records we found over 60% of the arrests and almost all of the repeat arrest lived within a mile of the fair grounds.

Now the fair is rated as one of the 100 thing you must see in the country.

We would bill the Fair for all overtime, meals, uniform cleaning (one day was all a uniform lasted waking around in the heat) and lodging for troopers who came in from all over the state.

A testimonial of how well we did. The last year I worked the fair I arrested a drunk and his sober friend said "I told him if you go to the fair and get drunk and they will throw your ass in jail so fast, I told him"

My Most Unusual Thank You Letter

Iowa Department of Public Safety
Des Moines, Ia 50309

Ref: Officer Black – Iowa Highway Patrol
Dear Sir:

It has been many years, but Officer Black's name and your Highway Patrol is still thought of fondly by myself and my family.

About June of 1971 my family of four young children, my wife and myself were traveling across Iowa and as we approached Des Moines on I-80, were involved in a serious auto crash. The Highway Patrol responded very quickly and we were just amazed. Officer Black questioned all of us at the hospital; Helped arrange for a motel; and gave us assistance in locating our destroyed vehicle and transported us to a motel. He even called the next day to see if we needed additional help.

I'd just like to say thanks to Officer Black and your Department for the help rendered and commends all of you for an excellent department.
Sincerely
Clifford J. Daly

The unusual part about this letter is it was written Nov. 23, 1981 over ten years after the crash.

Animal Heads

One of the Patrol's former duties was to transport the heads of animals that had bitten a person to the Iowa State Veterinary Lab in Ames where they tested it for rabies. The two requirements were that the head had to be removed by a veterinarian, who completed a form certifying that the animal had bitten a person. Since these were relayed from all over the state, it created some interesting incidents. For example, in one case the animal was a cow and the head was transported in a wash tub packed with ice.

Another case involved a shoe box containing a mouse that had bitten its owner. When the patrolman got to Ames, he found a hole in the box and no mouse. The vet had placed the live mouse in the box, so naturally the prisoner chewed a hole in the box and escaped. Now, the idea of a live, possibly rabid, mouse loose in your patrol car would make one nervous at best. The patrolman parked his car and got several mouse traps. After setting them at strategic points inside his car, he left for a few hours and returned to find the mouse dead in a trap. (I hope it was the correct mouse.) He put it in the box and left it at the Lab.

But my best animal head story is when I was called by a city police officer to pick up a raccoon head to deliver to Ames. When I met him I asked out of curiosity who had been bitten.

"No one," he replied, "this raccoon had been between two houses staggering around." He had shot it with his pistol. I told him that it was required for the animal to have bitten a person and for a vet to have filled out the paperwork and removed the head.

"Well, what should I do with the body?" the officer asked.

We opened the trunk of his police car to get it out and — surprise! — it wasn't dead. It couldn't get out of the trunk, but had moved to the front area where it lay there snarling at us, showing its sharp teeth.

Now the police officer was really concerned and asked, "What do I do with it now?"

"For one thing," I advised, "don't shoot it where it is or the bullet will end up in the gas tank." Finally, I had him drive out behind the city garage, so no one would see me beating a sick raccoon with a crowbar in the trunk of a police car.

Black Is Back

After 31 years, the Iowa State Patrol is returning to black patrol cars. From the Patrol's founding in 1935 through 1967 all patrol cars were black, except for a one-year trial of assorted-colored cars in 1961. In 1968, they changed to white. In 1985, the white cars were replaced with gold cars in honor of the Patrol's 50th anniversary.

In 1998, the order was placed for 75 black patrol cars and, for the first time, the markings on the cars were changed. A gold stripe now runs the length of the car. The Patrol shield has been reduced in size and moved to the rear fender, replacing the large shield on the door.

Color was not the only change in 1968. Until that time, the Patrol purchased cars as cheaply as possible: the lowest-priced body style, three-speed manual transmissions, no power steering, no power brakes, no radio, and no extras. While this reduced the purchase price, it also greatly reduced the resale price. Who wanted a car with no extras? In 1968, Ford patrol cars had automatic transmissions, power steering, radios, and air conditioning. When those cars were sold, they brought back twice what was spent for the extras.

At that time, the used cars were sold on a sealed bid system. A bidder picked up a list of all the cars the state had for sale, wrote in his bid, and turned it in. The bids were opened and the highest bid on each car was accepted. It was possible to pick up a list and make very low bids on all the cars and occasionally get one. This system has been changed to a public auction and the cars

The problems with the black cars, the black absorbed heat in the summer, and they were hard to keep clean. When it was time to turn them and the garage took of the decals you could see the outline of them in the paint that was protected by the decals.

We went back to gold cars.

No I Will Walk Him Back

I was working the evening shift at the Iowa State Fair. As I walked through the midway, I was approached by the manager. He told me of a man who was stealing prizes from the games. He would go up to the game, grab a prize and run away. He had done this in the afternoon, but had eluded the day shift Troopers. He told me they had seen him back again.

Just then, one of the workers pointed and said, "There he is." My partner and I started toward him and he took off running. I decided to chase him and told my partner to call the area car to come assist. At that time I was doing a lot of running, but not with a gun belt and all the equipment, body armor, and street shoes. I thought if I could just keep him in sight until the car got there, we could catch him. So I set a pace I could handle.

We ran down a busy street, passing fair goers heading in and out of the fair. I realized I was keeping up. As we approached the gate, I yelled at the attendant to close it, but he just looked at us as we ran by, out the gate and into the parking lot. Now I was starting to gain on him. Near the end of the parking lot, he just stopped and stood there gasping for air. I caught up and assisted him to the vertical arrest position. When the area car finally arrived, they asked, "Do you want a ride back with the prisoner?"

I answered, "No, all the people who saw me go by chasing him are going to see me walking him back." And they did.

Is He Dead?

It is four AM and I have a body lying alongside Interstate 35 under the Highway 210 overpass. Let me tell you how it got there and the problems I had getting it removed from the scene.

The story begins with a semi traveling southbound on I-35. The engine stalls and by the time the driver realizes it won't restart, he's going too slow to get the truck and trailer completely off the pavement and onto the shoulder. The trailer ends up setting in the outside lane on the interstate.

A second semi sees him stop and pulls over onto the shoulder ahead of him. The two drivers from that semi start walking back to see if they can help. They all walk to the rear of the stalled truck and notice that it has no taillights. As they are discussing this, a third semi is coming down the road right at them. Two of the drivers jump left and one jumps to the right – a fatal mistake for the driver who jumps to the right. He is hit by the semi and knocked onto the shoulder between two pillars of the overpass before semi number three slams into the rear of the stalled truck. His load of steel manhole covers goes flying down the highway like so many large poker chips littering the highway. It's a traffic mess.

Shortly after I get there to help divert traffic, the ambulance arrives. As soon as the body is measured and photographed, I tell the ambulance driver they can take the body to the hospital/morgue. The new volunteer fire chief/ambulance driver tells me he can't tie up his ambulance by hauling dead bodies – that he has to be available to transport the living. Great! A new chief who wants to show his authority and how important his ambulance is to his small town.

I call for a hearse.

The man answering the phone at the funeral home asks if the body has been pronounced dead by the medical examiner. Since it hasn't, he can't transport the body. Personally, I just think he doesn't want to get up and come out on a cold night. Okay, no problem. We'll just call the medical examiner. But I have the feeling this is not the end of my problems. I cover the body and begin the paperwork.

The assistant medical examiner arrives. He is Pakistani with poor English skills. I'm right, my problems have not ended. Our conversation goes like this:

Me: "I need for you to pronounce him dead."
Him: "You bring hospital. I do autopsy. Tell you cause.
Me: "Okay, I got that. But is he dead?"
Him: "You bring hospital. I do autopsy. Tell you."

Okay, this is not working. The ambulance won't haul him because he's dead, the hearse won't come until he is certified as dead. The assistant medical examiner wants to do an autopsy (not usually done on living people), but I can't get the body transported until he's pronounced dead. Time for a new approach. I *could* go over to the body and kneel down for thirty seconds and say, "I feel a pulse." Then the ambulance driver/fire chief would be afraid not to haul him if I insist, or else he'll get a lot of bad press. But I'd rather not get into a power struggle with them. The assistant medical examiner won't say he's dead – he just wants to do the autopsy.

I have an idea!I point to the body and ask the assistant medical examiner, "Is he alive? "Oh no, oh no, not alive," is the assistant medical examiner's response. Close enough! If I can't get "dead" I'll settle for "not alive."

Over the Sidewalk and Through the Hedge

When I first joined the Iowa Highway Patrol I was assigned as a Driver's License Examiner for a while. During that time, we were involved in some minor traffic accidents.

The applicants drove their own cars and I rode in the passenger seat, so there was no brake on my side of the car. One young lady was taking her driving test and, as we approached an intersection with a stop sign, she panicked and stepped on the accelerator pedal instead of the brake. By the time we got stopped, she had run over the curb, driven across the sidewalk, through a hedge and finally came to a stop crossways on the crossing street.

She turned to me and said, "I suppose this means I failed?"

For a brief moment I thought maybe I had better pass her or she would come back to try again, but did, in fact, have to fail her. When we got back to the office, after a few minutes her father came in demanding to know why I had failed her. I explained it to him and suggested he check the grill where he would find some of the hedge.

He said, "Sorry that is not what I was told".

Thank You for the Ticket

It is not often that a Trooper receives a letter thanking him or her for writing someone a traffic ticket. So I was surprised to receive a "thank you" letter from the mother of a young lady to whom I had written a seat belt citation.

The mother explained that the daughter had not been wearing her seat belt prior to the citation being issued, but afterward she had started wearing it. Her daughter had just been involved in a serious car accident and had received only minor injuries thanks to her wearing the seat belt. Her daughter's friend in the passenger seat had not been belted and was thrown into the windshield, suffering a concussion and severe facial cuts which were going to leave scars.

Her daughter was planning to become a fashion model and her mother was sure that had I not given her a ticket, she would also have been scarred for life.

The First Police Dog Leaves His Mark

The first police dog to arrive in central Iowa was owned by the local sheriff's department. The first time I got to see the animal work was during a building search. The burglar alarm was going off at one of the large furniture stores. The alarm company told us the owner was on the way. We secured outside until he arrived with the keys.

As you can imagine, a large store full of assorted furniture would be a difficult place to search - or the perfect place to use the new dog that was trained to perform building searches. The deputy was very proud of his dog, Hans, and this was their first chance to show off. When the owner unlocked the door, the deputy very proudly gave Hans the command to search. Hans entered the building, stopped about ten feet inside the door, squatted, and left a pile on the floor before proceeding to search the building.

While Hans was not embarrassed, the deputy was embarrassed enough for both of them. He kept saying, "He's never done that before; I'll clean it up."

Hans did a search of the building, but we didn't find anyone or any evidence of a break-in. The deputy knew that the story would not be of the building search, but that Hans had definitely left his mark on this case.

Eye Tests

For many years the Iowa Highway Patrol was responsible for the issuance of state driver's licenses. A Driver's Licensing Crew consisted of a Patrolman and two civilian clerks. Some of the crews worked in one permanent location in the bigger cities, while others moved daily to different locations for a week then repeated the pattern the following week. The crew worked five and one-half days a week including half-days on Saturdays. The Patrolman gave the driving behind-the-wheel examinations and, whenever possible, gave the clerks a break.

Those Saturdays were never "half-days" in reality for the crews. There was a line of applicants from when they first opened in the morning and just as big a line at noon when the crew crowded them inside, locked the doors, finished them up by one or one-thirty, then balanced the books, and deposited the money. I would get home about three PM. I was assigned to a permanent location in Des Moines where we had some memorable experiences.

Once a man came in who could not pass the vision test to renew his license. He became very angry, insisting there was nothing wrong with his eyes. He became more belligerent blaming the machine and demanding a new test. I gave him a form to take to his eye doctor to check his vision and verify his visual acuity. He threw the paper on the floor. I told him to pick it up and leave or I would arrest him. He finally picked up the paper and stomped out, slamming the door on his way. A week later he came back with his vision slip and a pair of glasses. He apologized profusely and told me his eye doctor told him if he'd waited much longer, he would have lost his sight.

If an applicant wore glasses, I always asked him or her if they would like to try it without their glasses. I asked, "Would you like to try this without your glasses?" One man replied: "No, I couldn't drive without my glasses. In fact, if I didn't have my glasses, I couldn't find my car." You can't argue with that.

On another occasion a man came in to renew his license as I was giving the clerks a break. When I checked his license it showed him to be a white male with blue eyes. The man standing before me was a black male with brown eyes. I took him into the office and soon he admitted he was renewing the license for a friend who could not pass the vision test. He said his friend was waiting outside in a red 1965 Chevy. I walked outside to find the car. The driver's eyesight was bad enough that he did not see me coming until it was too late. I arrested both of them and suspended the man with poor eyesight's driver's license on the spot.

I wondered what would make one think it was a good idea to get a driver's license for someone who could not see well enough to pass the vision test.

It Does Not Effect Anyone Else

One of the arguments I hear when the seat belt law and motorcycle helmet was: It's my body and it is my decision and it does not affect anyone else.

I would answer with this;

You are the person I have been looking for.

When I have to go to a home to tell someone one of their family has just been killed in an accident I want you to come along.

It would make it so much easier for me to have you explain to them how they are not affect.

When the mother or father says "we have 4 children what am I going to do?

How do I take care of them"?

You can explain how the decision to not wear a seat belt or helmet was his decision and she and the kids are not affected.

When the parents are in shock, when the kids are crying and when I don't know what to say.

I will say just "this guy will explain how you are not affected".

Now If I can get you name and phone number it will help me a lot.

I was giving a safety talk one day to a group and the guy actually ran out the door when I asked for his name and phone number.

Nighttime Illuminating Flare

It was the night before a large rock concert in Des Moines and many of those attending were camping in the state park. Of course, they were drinking and playing music way too loud for the other campers who were trying to sleep. When the park ranger asked them to quiet down, they refused. The ranger then ordered the rowdies out of the park. Again, they refused – this time in a very rude manner. That's when the ranger called us for assistance.

At about one AM, troopers and sheriff deputies who were on duty in the county responded. There were no lights in the camping area. We talked to the ranger, then all proceeded to the camping area. Using the public address system on his patrol car, the ranger once again ordered the troublemakers to leave the park. Again, there was a rude answer from the rowdies from out of the darkness. Some people get brave when they think you can't see them.

I had a friend in the National Guard and he sometimes supplied us with military equipment. So, I had some military pop-up nighttime illuminating flares from him – the type you see in war movies to light up a battlefield. I thought this would be a great place to use one, so I did.

When you set one off, it makes a loud boom as it launches the flare, then the flare ignites high up, then floats down on a small parachute. It lights up the area like daylight.

I set it off and it worked great. It made a boom when I fired it, them a pop and the whole area was lit up. Now we could see the rowdies very well. They were standing with their mouths open pointing up at the flare. The noise stopped and they started packing up to leave.

One of the deputies came up to me and said, "Next time you do that, tell us before you do. It scared the hell out of me!"

It Takes a Licking

Troopers sometimes display a dark sense of humor, if they did not do something to break the tension it could get to them. The average person does not understand this so you have to be careful when you do it.

On a two lane stretch of highway at 3AM on a warn summer night an intoxicated driver crosses the center line and sideswipes a UPS semi. The driver has her arm out the window and it is cut off and as the car hits the trailer she is killed.

Trooper and fire personnel work to get the body out and note the missing arm. Myself and another trooper take our flashlights and walk the edges of the road looking for the arm.

I find it and note a wristwatch is still on the arm. As I return to the group I hold up the arm and say, "It's true, they do take a licking and keep on ticking". Just as a new crew pulls up, had they been 30 second sooner I would not had a chance to use that old joke.

The cops and firemen laughed, and some stress was relieved.

Until I had to go tell the family.

Prison Riot

During a nice sunny day while working I was ordered to report to the office ASAP. I overheard all the other cars working ordered to come to the office

ASAP or call in depending on how close they were to the office. I wondered what is this all about?

When I arrived at the office I was met by the

Lieutenant who informed me "Go home, pack a bag for 3 or 4 days, come back here, pair up and head for the prison at Fort Madison Red Lights and siren on.

There is a riot going on."

I rushed home, packed, told my wife where I was going and left leaving a worried wife behind.

I paired up with another trooper and we hit the interstate, flipped on the lights and siren and headed for the prison.

The prison at Fort Madison holds the men serving life without parole inmates, violent prisoners as well as the rest of the population. People who have nothing to loose or ones who don't care. Not a place you want to visit.

When we arrived at the prison we went to the gathering area and were told the prisoners had taken several guards hostage and had killed at least one the other prisoners. We were to stand by as they were trying to contact the prisoners and see what they wanted.

This went on for several hours. During this time the prisoners had gotten a fork truck out of the furniture shop and were trying to break into the protective custody section. Fortunately they failed or there would have been more murders as that houses the snitches and child molesters etc.

The negotiations obtained the release of the guards.

Finally we were told we were going in.

Some one had decided we could not take our pistols in with us and only one trooper would be armed with a shotgun. The rest would carry riot batons. Not a popular decision with us going in.

We were in groups of eight consisting of 7 troopers and one prison guard. The layout of the prison was not know to us so the guard was very useful.

I was assigned to cell block number seven which we found was where they kept the most violent prisoners.

One of the worst feelings of my life was when the first gate locked and closed behind me and I waited for the second gate to open. We could only go in 16 men at a time. I was with the second group to go through the gates and that was fine with me not being first. Then to step out into the prison yard and look at those high stone walls was spooky. I had not had claustrophobia until then. I knew a quick exit or quick reinforcements was not possible. We were on our own and we were out numbered in there. I knew this might not end well.

As we started across the open area to the cell block we were accompanied by a verbal assault from the prisons questioning our parenthood and sexual orientation. As we got closer, one of the inmates came down from the steps to confront us. The guard with us said "watch this guy he has a black belt and has hurt several other inmates".

He approached us yelling at us "what are you doing here. We will kick your ass" while his friends watched for the steps to see how we reacted.

He stopped about 20 feet away and continued to run his mouth. While he was so busy trying to impress his friends he failed to notice a trooper carrying a shotgun had walked around behind him. Finally he was told to turn around and put his hand behind his back. At that he jumped into a fighting stance and put is hand up while inviting us to try it. BIG MISTAKE. The trooper behind him stepped forward and popped him in the head with the shotgun butt.

He went down like a sack of potatoes. If you know anything about head cuts they look much worse than they are blood wise.

The cell block went silent. All the background noise from the prisoners stopped.

We stepped over the prone form of Black Belt Guy and ordered the rest to come down, lay prone with their hand behind their backs. They all complied.

They knew the prison guards and what to expect but not us and Black Belt Guy was their test. If he had managed to intimidate us we would have had a very hard time.

Going into the next cell block the prisoners in there were yelling, throwing stuff from the their cells and destroying whatever they could. The Sgt told the troopers with the shotguns to empty the chambers on of the guns. Then when we stepped into the cell block he had us chamber a round in our shotguns. If you have ever heard that sound you will always recognize it. The crack of that action reverberated off the cell block walls and instantly it got real quiet in there.

We spent the next 2 days moving prisoners out of one building to the cells in another, searching the cells and moving them back. It went fairly well.

There was no resistance but a lot of complaining by the convicts. While searching cells I had only one convict say he would not come out. There were 3 of us. Myself, my partner and the prison guard. I could see the convict get ready to fight. He clenched his fists and took the fighting stance. I looked at my partner and indicated I would go high and he would go low. I then turned to look at the inmate and started to grin. The inmate looked at me and then my partner. We just stared back. He then looked at the guard who gave him a quick nod. The inmate got a puzzled look on his face and then backed out of stance and complied with our orders.

I still have a homemade knife from the prison. It is made from two, 4 inch steel slats welded together then shaped and sharpened on a grinder. My partner has a hammer. How did they managed to make the knife and get it to cell as well as a hammer?

None of us were injured in this and I am sure it was because of that first encounter with Black Belt Guy.

When we were released and as I went out the gates I turned and looked back at those high gray walls. I could feel the tension finally leaving my body.

I thought if you want to scare someone into going straight take him in there for a day.

While on the subject of the prison there is a funny story the warden told us. The prison has an auto- body shop where they learn to repair and restore cars and trucks. The warden had purchased an old pickup truck. He brought it to the shop to be restored. He had to pay the cost of supplies and labor.

When the restoration was finished he picked up the truck. He knew the inmates would have to do something to sabotage the truck. Nothing fatal, but something. As soon as he picked it up he took it to a garage and had it inspected. They found nothing out of order.

The warden drove it a few days. It was when he pulled in to buy gas he found what the inmates had done.

The inmates has welled the gas cap on. He could not get it off to put gas in the tank.

True State Trooper Stories

Troopers Charles Black and David Kopp leaving the Fort Madison Penitentiary after the riot was controlled. Note the smiles of relief.

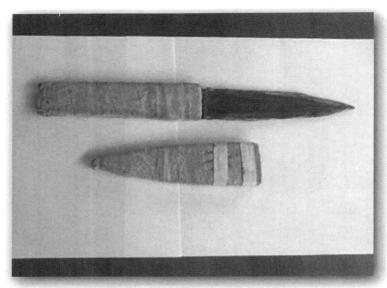

The knife mentioned in the story

I Just Called His Bluff

He was not a tough guy but he had a habit of getting arrested in the local bars for one thing or another but never for fighting.

When arrested he would wait till you got him handcuffed and then he would start running his mouth.

He would make it loud enough so everyone in the bar could hear him. "If I did not have these cuffs on I would kick your ass" or "If it wasn't for that badge and gun you are a bunch of cowards". Of course, his language was much more colorful and profane.

Finally one night near end of shift I arrested him in a bar. Some other troops arrived and he started it again loudly "If you did not have that badge and gun and took these cuffs off I would kick your ass".

I was really tired of this. I took my hat off handed it to one of the troops, then removed my badge followed by my gun belt. When he saw this he asks

What are you doing". I replied "Just what you wanted; no badge no gun and this trooper is going to take your cuffs off".

The trooper holding my equipment asked "Sarge are you sure about this".

I knew this story would get around and the Captain would not be pleased, but he had had similar experiences. I expected to get chewed out good but it was going to be worth it. Plus I was pretty sure Big Mouth was not going to fight. Big mouth looked scared now. When the trooper approached him with the handcuff key he said "You can't do this".

The Trooper replied "Just watch me".

The biggest struggle of the night was with Big Mouth trying keep the trooper from unlocking his cuffs.

The bar crowd was starting to laugh. I told the trooper to stop. I asked Big Mouth loud enough for all to hear.

"What was all that talk about kicking my ass? Did you do it because you felt safe with the cuffs on". He mumbled "Yes". I replied "I can't hear you I want you to say it loud enough for everyone to hear it or the cuffs come off". He spoke right up with a louder and more resounding "Yes".

As expected, when I came to work the next evening I was instructed to go see the Captain. He asked what happened and I told him. He told me that was not procedure and I could consider this an oral reprimand.

Then he told me a couple of stories about his experiences and I went back to work.

I think I heard him chuckling when I left.

The Phone Call

I had a phone call at 1:30 AM of course, you always worry, since a late-night call is not usually good news. It went like this:

Me: Hello
Him: I know you're sleeping with my girl friend.
Me: What?
Him: I know you're sleeping with my girl friend.
Me: You have the wrong number.
Him: No. I know you're sleeping with my girl friend.
Me: You have the wrong number.
Him: Don't B.S. me.
Me: I'll tell you something. I'm almost seventy years old and I do appreciate the compliment. If she is sleeping with me, she's no longer your girlfriend, and if a seventy-year-old man can steal your girlfriend, then how lame are you?

He hung up.

I went back to bed and my wife Trudy said, "Who was that?" I said, "Your boyfriend, I guess. I'll tell you in the morning. She said, "No, you will tell me now!" And I did.

The Blessed Virgin

This did not happen to me but to fellow Trooper Ron Reid and is to good not to pass on.

It is a few days before Christmas and we are working the night shift. He is driving up the highway northbound when a car drives out of the Victoria

Lodge parking lot and heads south. As the trooper watched this car crossed both southbound lanes and is driving southbound in the median. The trooper turns around and pulls up behind this car. The driver is still going south in the median and is paying no attention to the trooper or the flashing lights.

The trooper decides to try a different approach. He turns his spotlight on the car and uses the loud speaker to tell the Median Driver to stop his car. The car stops immediately.

When the trooper gets to the car the Median Driver is drunk and in tears.

The trooper asks what is going on.
The driver asks "Did you see her"?
The trooper asks "See who"?

The driver replies "The Blessed Virgin Mary. She appeared in a burst of light and told me to stop right here".

My guess is that may be the one and only time a trooper has ever been mistaken for the Blessed
Virgin Mary.

Bozo the Clown

Hard as it may be to believe, troopers do play jokes on each other – especially on the new troopers. I was working the Iowa State Fair with a new female trooper who is as nice a person as you could ever meet, and is still a special friend. However, that year on the state fair midway was a new attraction: Bozo the Clown.

Bozo sat in a dunk tank, the one where you throw balls at a target that, when hit, dunks the sitter from his perch and into the water. Bozo would sit up there and insult people as they walked by, encouraging them to pay a dollar for three balls to try to dunk him. He was very good at the insults. Here are some examples:

"Hey, you with the yellow shirt and the teeth to match."

"Lady, what are you doing with that guy? Did you lose a bet?"

"Hey, ugly! I bet they had to tie a pork chop around your neck just to get the dog to play with you."

So we talked to Bozo and set it up so when I came around with her he would start insulting her. He didn't disappoint:

"Hey, lady trooper, what happened? Did the whole troop, troop on your face? Did your gun backfire?"

She was just stunned for a minute trying to figure out how to react. She turned to look at me for any ideas and when she saw the three of us laughing so hard, it dawned on her what had happened. She handled it well.

Well, we thought this had worked so well and been so much fun, we would try it again. This time we picked as our target a trooper who thought very well of himself and who was very proud of his mustache. We thought we had a great target.

When we walked by the dunk tank, Bozo started: "Hey, Trooper, what's that brown stuff on your lip? Did something fly up while you were chasing a guy through the cattle barn? How bad does it smell?"

Up until then we were having a great time, but that changed quickly. Our targeted colleague started toward the back of the dunk tank vowing to "explain some things to that smart-mouthed son of a . . ." We had to chase him down to stop him and explain what was going on. We managed to get him stopped, but he saw no humor in it.

We Did.

The new Lady Trooper in this story became a writer of romance novels. In one of the books she used Bozo the Clown and dedicated the book in part to me. It Went

"Thanks, too, to retired Iowa State Patrol Sergeant Charlie Black, ex-ISP 336, my first State Patrol Field training officer, for giving me a "behind the scenes" introduction to the Iowa State Fair--including an up close and personal encounter with "The Great Bozo"--as a rookie trooper way back when. Those experiences proved, uh, helpful in crafting this story. I still owe you one, Chuck, you dog.

Fickle Fate

After 35 years as a State Trooper. I have seen a lot of things and I have learned just how fickle fate can be.

I have seen people loose control of their cars and run through the median and across three lanes of busy oncoming traffic and not get hit. And I have seen a county blacktop road on early Sunday morning with one car every 5 minutes. A southbound car drifts off onto the shoulder and jerks back too hard. The car crosses the road into the path of the only vehicle within 5 miles and is struck. The driver of that vehicle is killed. If he had stopped to tie his shoe before he got in a van he would have been the 3 or 4 seconds behind and would be alive. If he had buckled his seat belt he would be alive.

Two days later I get called to an accident on Interstate Highway 80. It is the middle of the afternoon heavy traffic. A car going west loses control goes into the medial up across 3 lanes of traffic and does not get touched before he goes into the ditch.

Fate can be fickle.

Secret Service Protection

Did you ever wonder how the candidates qualify for Secret Service protection

In order for a candidate to qualify for the protection, they must meet these guidelines:

The candidate must have publicly announced their candidacy.

The candidate must be entered in at least 10 primaries.

The candidate must be seeking the nomination of a party who received at least 10% of the popular vote in the last election.

The candidate must qualify for matching funds of at least $100,000.

The candidate must register at least 5% in the polls conducted by ABC,

CBS, NBC and CNN or receive 10% of the votes in two consecutive primaries.

Protection is provided only while the candidate is in the United States.

The Motorcycle Toss

I was one of the first bunch of Troopers to be trained as a Technical Accident Investigator by the State Patrol. As part of the training we took patrol cars that had been turned in and were awaiting being auctioned off. We went to a large parking lot we would slam on the brakes at a known speed and leave skid marks. We would then use these skids to figure the speed of the car and match it to the known speed. This way if we were challenged in court we could testify that we knew the formulas worked. But we or no one else had much information on motorcycles sliding on their sides. We figured out a way to have some fun collecting that information.

Our Vehicle theft unit had just broken up a motorcycle theft ring and some of the cycles they had recovered had had the Vehicle Identification

Number (VIN) could not be identified and returned.

They could not be sold without the VIN numbers so had to be sent to the crusher. We came up with a use for them before they were crushed. Using a pickup truck from the patrol garage we would load a motorcycle, get the truck up to a known speed and throw a motorcycle out the back. It would slide down the road and we could measure how far it went and calculate the speed. We used the roads at Camp Dodge Military Base as it had pavement, gravel, black top, dirt roads and not much traffic. We would be able to collect information on all surface types. In the end we had very good statistics on skid resistance on a down motorcycle.

I am sure the people who saw us loading a motorcycle into the truck, get going, throw it out, stop, load it up and do it again must have thought we were crazy.

Darrell and the Pig

One of the small towns in my area, like many Iowa small towns, has a highway running through it. The police force consisted of one officer, Officer Darrell. Since this town was not willing to pay much for an officer, they did not get the sharpest knife in the drawer.

One day, as a truck hauling big sow pigs to market passed through town, a large sow fell out of the truck onto the highway. I have no idea how it fell out and the driver did not notice, as he never returned looking for it. The pig was skinned up a bit, though not seriously injured. However, that pig was in one bad mood. Officer Darrell was sent to handle the situation.

I happened to be in the area and drove over to see if he needed any help. When I pulled up I saw Darrell on the hood of his car, service pistol drawn, with a bloody pig trying to climb up after him. When he first pulled up, Darrell had tried to herd the pig, but it refused to move. So, Darrell decided to shoot the pig with his 9 mm, but he was shooting it in the body, which, on a fat hog, does not work. All he did was make it really mad. The pig charged him and

Darrell ran and jumped on the hood of his car. That was the situation as I arrived on the scene.

Once I finally quit laughing, I got out of my car, took my shotgun and mercifully killed the sow, thereby rescuing Dean from his assailant. Dean then wanted to know what to do with the pig. As much lead as he had put in it, I suggested he call Rudolph and Ralph, who are brothers who specialize in road kill . . . but that's another story.

Push Bumpers

The Patrol had just received new light bars for the patrol cars. In addition to being brighter lights on smaller bars, these units included an air horn along with the standard siren. I was one of the first troopers to get one of these. At the time I was also testing the first and only set of push bumpers the Patrol ever bought.

Dwight was one of the troopers at our post. He was a tall, nervous young man who had more than his share of bad luck. One night as I was driving down Second Avenue, I saw that Dwight had a car stopped and was in his patrol car writing out a ticket. The urge was too strong not to pull something on him, so I turned off my lights and rolled up behind him slowly on the shoulder. Just as I bumped him with the push bumpers I hit the air horn. I thought he was going to get whiplash as fast as his head turned to see what happened. When he saw it was me, he jumped out of his car and came running back. I put my car in reverse and backed down the shoulder with him chasing me, shaking his fist and saying unprintable things.

He was as honest and sincere a man as you would ever meet, but bad luck just seemed to follow him. One time he stopped a car whose driver had a suspended license. The guy pleaded with Dwight not to tow his car – that his wife would come and get it. Being a nice guy, Dwight told him okay, but that he (Dwight) would have to drive the car off the road until the guy's wife could come and get it. The driver failed to mention that the car had no brakes and Dwight rolled it into a garage.

Another time Dwight's patrol car was broken down, so he was using his captain's car. Dwight's brother's car wouldn't start, so Dwight decided to give the car a push to start it. However, his brother braked suddenly at the wrong time causing front end damage on the captain's car. The Captain was not a happy camper.

Still another time, the D.O.T. was installing a new shoulder along the highway. They had removed the old shoulder which left a one-foot drop at the edge of the roadway, which they marked with cones. A semi driver got his wheels over the edge of the pavement cutout and the truck ended up on its side. The truck had to be unloaded which took most of the day. Meanwhile, the D.O.T. workers were spreading new concrete to fill in the shoulder. When it was time to right the truck, we were called for traffic control. Dwight was one of the cars called to assist. Approaching the scene, Dwight drove onto the fresh concrete, sinking in and becoming stuck. The tractor that had been helping to unload the truck pulled him out and we sent him straight to the D.O.T. shop to use the pressure washer to get the wet concrete off the car before it hardened. Since the cement was fresh, I it was easy to fix. Once again Dwight was driving another troopers car.

I am in the front row left end.

STATE OF IOWA :
: SS.
COUNTY OF POLK :

I, Charles A. Black, do solemnly swear that I will support the Constitution of the United States, and the Constitution of the State of Iowa, and that I will faithfully and impartially, to the best of my ability, discharge all of the duties of the Office as Patrolman of the Iowa Highway Safety Patrol of the Department of Public Safety of the State of Iowa, as now or hereafter required by law, so help me God.

CHARLES A. BLACK

Subscribed and sworn to before me this 26th day of May, 1965.

William F. Sueppel, Commissioner

Oath of office and my first I.D. card

1961 Ford

My first patrol car. It was used. It had a 390 cu. in. engine, 3 speed manual transmission with overdrive but had no Air Conditioning.

1964 Ford

My second patrol car. When the Chief saw me driving the blue 1961 Ford he told supply to issue me different car. I got a used car again but newer.

1965 Chevy

My first new car in front of our first house.

True State Trooper Stories

1995 Chevy

The best patrol car I ever had. It would do 140 mph and instead of lifting at that speed it stayed solid. It was the best bad road car also.

Sgt. Charles A Black

I came up with the idea for this poster and persuaded the governor's Traffic SafetyBureau to pay for it.
L to R Trooper Sue Bulver, Myself, Trooper Jim Saunders

True State Trooper Stories

Using my patrol car to tow an airplane off the interstate. He ran out of fuel and was forced to land there. Trooper/pilot Gary Herrick stands on the airplane wing giving directions to the pilot.

Iowa State Fair Night shift: 38 troopers and 2 Sgts. In the golf cart L to R myself and Sgt. Mark Probst

The Life Flight helicopter and 3 flight nurses. Not a better crew to work with.

An unhappy customer

True State Trooper Stories

I love this job!

Made in the USA
Lexington, KY
08 November 2016